Are You Ready to Quit Smoking?
The Book That Prepares You for Quitting, Supports You as You Take Action, and Encourages You as You Become an Ex-Smoker!

Linda R. Bryson

Stop-Smoking Program
Good Samaritan Hospital
Corvallis, Oregon

Kendall/Hunt
Publishing Company
Dubuque, Iowa

Contents

Acknowledgments

To my husband Bill—for his constructive criticism and his unlimited patience when there was only "manuscript" for dinner.

To my entire family and three daughters—for loving, caring, and being there.

To my Father, Robert W. Henderson—for author's photograph.

To Jay Barton—for his photography in Young Adult Chapter.

To Health Educator Merrie Ziady—for her contributions and for her dedicated work in smoking cessation and stress management.

To Cartoonist Craig Parish—for his insightful and creative talent.

To my friend and manuscript typist Donna Lee Norvell-Race—for her creative and interpretive spirit.

To Editors Sue Mason and Bev McFarland—for helping me to remain grammatically correct while "talking on paper."

To the staff and physicians at Good Samaritan Hospital in Corvallis, Oregon—for caring enough about people and the quality of life to create and support a stop-smoking program.

To the SMOKERS and EX-SMOKERS I have known—for teaching me most of what I know in helping people to become successful ex-smokers.

Paper Lady Blues

Paper Lady, when are you going to let me go?
You've been my friend so long,
But your faults are starting to show.

Paper Lady, I never cared you were there—
But let me go now,
You're getting on my nerves,
And my clothes, and my hair.

Paper Lady, you tire me out when I walk
And Paper Lady, you interfere when I talk;
You've got control of my mind and my lungs,
Paper Lady, please quit dancing on my tongue.

You were my lover,
My friends thought you were cool.
Where are those friends now, you've got me hooked now,
And I feel like a fool.

And when I need you
I shake and come unglued.
Paper Lady, those are the smoking blues.

You clog my arteries
And massacre my lung sacs,
Paper Lady, please quit dancing on my back.

And let me go now;
I can do it alone,
I want my mind back,
Before it turns to stone.

Goodbye Lady, it's been ten days.
The memories linger
In many different ways.
Goodbye Lady, the air it smells so fine,
Goodbye Lady, you ain't no friend of mine!
And I can't lose,
I can't lose,
'Cause—I've lost the Paper Lady Blues.

Linda Bryson,
© 1979

How to Use This Workbook

I. Read the "INTRODUCTION" and "WHY DIDN'T I MAKE IT THE OTHER TIMES?" first.

II. Read "PREPARATION FOR QUIT DAY." Next, set your "quit date"—write it on the calendar in red ink, and get a good mind-set going for quitting.

III. Take the SMOKER'S TEST before you quit. Do your cigarette wrap sheet for one full day before you quit. Both of these exercises help to analyze your smoking routine so you can better prepare your battle plan or strategy. Write down your likes and dislikes.

IV. Read "ACTUAL WITHDRAWAL FROM NICOTINE." Practice the breathing and relaxation exercise or purchase a good relaxation tape to play daily. *Stock up on all substitutes that sound good to you.*

V. Be sure your family, friends, and co-workers read "HOW FAMILY, FRIENDS, AND CO-WORKERS CAN HELP." You need an educated support system.

VI. "QUIT DAY." Start reading or rereading the remaining chapters. Keep the book handy so you can use it for reference, support and comfort at <u>any</u> time. *Reach for the book rather than a cigarette.*

I
Introduction

"Only by truly understanding the habit can we let it go."—L. B.

"Only by accepting that nicotine has control of us, do we gain back our control over nicotine."—L. B.

Why am I writing a book on how to become a SUCCESSFUL EX-SMOKER? Because I was a dedicated smoker . . . because I sincerely care about helping smokers to quit smoking, if and when they <u>choose</u> to quit. Anyone can quit smoking. I quit smoking twenty-seven times; but I only <u>stayed</u> off one time—the last time.

First, let me define a successful ex-smoker. He or she is the smoker who has quit smoking <u>without</u> picking up the negative side-effects of SELF-RIGHTEOUSNESS, OBESITY or MEANNESS. Many ex-smokers exhibit at least one of these undesirable side-effects. In fact, I doubt if they have really stopped smoking—they have just stopped the physical act of "lighting up." However, in their hearts, they emotionally seem to be smoking—they resent any living beings who still have the nerve to admit they enjoy their smoking. They just exchanged one negative habit for another. This book is about exchanging a negative habit for some new positive habits.

Quitting smoking has to be the smoker's own decision. If someone cared enough about you to give you this book, read it and then make your decision to quit now or to set a later quit date. People nagging at you is <u>not</u> positive reinforcement. If nagging worked, nagging clinics would be springing up all over the nation.

Why do I like smokers? Because they are interesting people! Non-smokers may consider them stupid, but I don't. I was not stupid to smoke cigarettes. I was only ignorant in thinking that something so much fun and relaxing would not end up so ADDICTIVE and COMPELLING. Besides, I had to be intelligent to think up the rationale that allowed me to continue smoking ten years after the surgeon general's initial report came out in 1964. I quit smoking twenty-seven times in my fifteen years of career smoking. Each time I quit, I always knew I would go back to smoking, and I did. The last time I quit, something was <u>different</u>. What was different? My attitude and my thinking processes. This is what I want to share with you in the book. I care about your becoming a successful ex-smoker.

After quitting smoking in 1974, I started conducting stop-smoking programs in our community on a volunteer basis. I am now working as a professional stop-smoking consultant for our local hospital. Most of what I have learned is <u>not</u> from reading, continuing my education, or research. I have learned from the smokers and ex-smokers I have met—I will always be grateful to them.

They realized that their smoking habit was the most important and time-consuming act they performed. So they changed their priorities. They changed their attitudes. And they learned to feel comfortable and proud with a new thinking process. The ones who were willing to <u>maintain</u>

*Please read, "A New Note on the Concept of Self-Righteousness (Page 95).

this attitudinal change are still successful ex-smokers. The others will make it—the time just wasn't right then. And the ones who made it are strong enough to know they are only in control if they can accept the fact that nicotine controls them. Sound like a contradiction? Not really—if you can't accept that addictive habits and drugs are strong characters, then you'll have to let them sneak up and attack you twenty-seven times before you start to believe it.

I've never read any other books on how to stop smoking. My education comes from my experience and from the experiences of hundreds of other smokers and ex-smokers. I thought if I read other books, I might feel compelled to write in an orderly, technical fashion. But SMOKERS ALREADY KNOW THE TECHNICALITIES OF SMOKING; WHAT THEY WANT TO LEARN IS HOW TO STOP SMOKING. So please try to become emotional with me. I will express my compassion, my anger, my emotions. I will not turn this book into a technical treadmill where we talk in theoretical circles and disregard the emotional aspects "as waste." I will not sweep the emotions under the pages. If this is done, then we assume that all it takes is intelligence to quit smoking. But—why then are intelligent people still smoking? The correct combination for quitting is to be intelligent, emotional, and aware. I've never decided who is more pathetic—a thinking person who has forgotten how to feel, or a feeling person who has forgotten how to think. It takes balance to win this game.

This book is not for "already perfect people." Perfect people already know it all and are incapable of learning, and growing, and changing. People who become successful ex-smokers are people who are able to accept their imperfections and not be intimidated by them. This book can also be applied to other addictions such as overeating, meanness, obesity, and self-righteousness. Success in any endeavor requires an attitude of positive thinking, which is what this book is all about.

This book will present ideas and tools to use. They are not new ideas and tools. They just get rediscovered every few hundred years by people who realize that they have worked since the beginning of time. And they get transferred back to the shelf when someone thinks they've discovered a new "magic" pill that works better. But they are tried and true, they worked for me, and I'm grateful that I rediscovered them in my life. However, if you don't use them, they will not work. You don't expect your car to work if you don't turn the key. Your iron will not heat if you don't plug it in. You've got to plug yourself in for success and set your ego on "automatic win".

This book is not for those people who only want to quit smoking, trade in their emotions, and pick up another habit—such as self-righteousness. I feel that self-righteous ex-smokers damage the stop-smoking cause more than cigarette advertising could ever hope to. As I said before, smokers are intelligent. And they are independent. A righteous ex-smoker only "ignites" the smokers' indignation to the point that they'll light up, if only in protest.

There are some rules to the stop smoking game that are listed on (page 4) . . . but here is the EMOTIONAL RULE of the game. It is the only rule that has to be followed at ALL TIMES to become a successful ex-smoker. If I say something that makes you feel very angry or defensive, please FEEL that way, and then figure out WHY. By standing back and looking at the angry you, you will discover a lot about yourself. Then you can turn that anger and defensiveness into positive energy for combatting the true enemy—NICOTINE.

If I sound self-righteous at times, forgive me. I AM NOT A PERFECT EX-SMOKER. I may seem to pat myself on the back too often for having given up the smoking habit, and you may resent this. Giving up cigarettes was the hardest thing I ever did in my life. Today, years

*Please read, "A New Note on the Concept of Self-Righteousness (Page 95).

later, people are <u>not</u> still surprised, or proud, or excited about the fact that I'm not smoking, but I am. I quit for myself, so "MYSELF" had better continue to pat me on the back. Nobody else will—GET USED TO THE IDEA OF PRAISING YOURSELF.

INITIALLY, you may stop smoking to please your family, friends, or co-workers, but if you want to <u>stay</u> off and be happy without cigarettes, you need to eventually be doing it for YOURSELF. This will be a natural transition; it will happen. So please allow me to pat myself and other ex-smokers on the back. We have all felt the pain, survived the pain, and only by sharing the rewards can we help you to quit smoking.

Please remember that if I make you feel angry, it's probably on purpose. Like the loving parent, I will often spout truths that are not appreciated or digested until later. You can only digest the truths as you <u>experience</u> them. DON'T GO AWAY ANGRY! It will be your loss not to experience the joy of giving up cigarettes.

If you are being forced into stopping smoking, and your attitude stinks at the moment, put the book aside for a short while. It will wait until you are motivated and you have had an attitude adjustment.

I really care about helping you quit smoking. Put as much effort into quitting smoking as you put into the smoking habit, and you'll come out a winner. It takes time, work, and money to smoke. Put time, work, and money into <u>quitting</u> the habit. Some of the ideas may seem crazy or foolish to you. But they may hit the right button for someone else. I'll throw out the ideas and you catch the ones that appeal to you. I am proud if I can become a part of helping you to achieve your own freedom.

Rules to the Stop-Smoking Game

1) Your determination to win must be at an all-time high.

2) Regaining control of your life must be the NUMBER ONE GOAL to win this game.

3) Preserving your good health must be your NUMBER TWO GOAL to win this game.

4) Family or friends cannot push you into playing this game—this is YOUR game.

5) You will allow yourself NO guilt feelings if at first you slip and have a cigarette—you will REPEAT to yourself, "I can beat this habit." There is no room for guilt—only determination to win—get back in the race!!

6) You must realize that it only takes ONE cigarette after you have won to force you to go back to "GO" and start all over again—Is it worth it?

7) That first cigarette you have after you have won the game is your biggest competitor. It knows that if you have that FIRST one again, you'll want that SECOND one, and eventually you'll become defeated—conquer it!!

8) When you first begin playing the "I Quit Smoking Game," try to avoid people who are still playing the "Smoking Game"—Take deep breaths when the urge for a cigarette hits you—take long walks or run in place—play the game in non-smoking areas.

9) PLEASE THINK OF YOURSELF AS AN EX-SMOKER. Keep reinforcing this idea.

II
"Why Didn't I Make It the Other Times?"

Chances are by the time you read this book, you've tried more than <u>one</u> time to quit. You may have even made it months or years before you gave in to that FIRST cigarette that seduced you into that SECOND cigarette. If you listened closely enough, you might have even heard NICOTINE chuckling as he enticed you back into his web of addiction. The tobacco industry is counting on you to stay addicted, so FIGHT BACK!

I know it isn't fair—the majority of drinkers can have an occasional drink without slipping into alcoholism, but less than ONE out of a HUNDRED smokers can have an occasional cigarette without becoming addicted all over again. It's not that we are WEAK. It is just a fact that nicotine is STRONG. This chapter lists some of the pitfalls that an ex-smoker can fall back into very easily. By identifying them, perhaps we can avoid them before they entrap us with our defenses down.

The Stress Express

There are certain incidents that are sure to trigger stress, even in the most confident and successful of ex-smokers. These are called the "biggies" like death, divorce, separation, job loss, or periods of depression and insecurity. How many of us slipped back to smoking after an argument with a spouse? (We proceeded to "show THEM" by having just one little cigarette!) Or how often will added pressures from a job or unusual family demands bring about added stress . . . and thoughts of a cigarette?

What we need to understand about these stress situations is that they can come on powerfully, unexpectedly, and with so much emotion that we can easily be knocked off the non-smoker's track if we don't recognize them as part of the STRESS EXPRESS.

Once we confront ourselves with the fact that there will always be stress, there will always be people dying, and there will always be situations where "life isn't fair," we can deal with not going back to smoking—not to having "just one little cigarette." One ex-smoker said that once she could accept these realities, her expectations of "how the world should be," and "how people should act" lessened when her expectations were not set unrealistically high. She was able to cope, and coping for some of us is surviving without cigarettes.

We need to remember that if someone we love dies, having a cigarette just <u>adds</u> the smoking problem to the sense-of-loss problem. If we are involved in a divorce, having a cigarette just <u>adds</u> to the separation problem. If we lose our job, having a cigarette just <u>adds</u> to the financial problem.

It really helped me to read Richard Bach's book, <u>Illusions</u>. It has a statement that reads, "You can't become disillusioned without an illusion". This statement is so simple, yet so profound. When we learn to view the world <u>without</u> unrealistic expectations, we are relieved of stress. When we learn to view people <u>without</u> unrealistic expectations, we are relieved of stress. Maybe the world and the people in it aren't perfect, BUT THEY ARE DOING THEIR BEST. And what more can we ask? If we don't ask for more, we are not as apt to become disillusioned enough to go back to smoking—as an excuse for being disillusioned! And we learn to take a deep breath, saying to ourselves, "O.K., so you've got ONE big problem, but if you take that first cigarette, you've then got TWO big problems, and who needs it?" Just three minutes later, we're so glad we made the decision NOT to smoke.

This isn't easy—it comes with practice—the SAME kind of practice that we were willing to give to the art of learning smoking. And when we can accept that the people around us and the world we live in are NOT revolving around us and OUR expectations, we learn to relax, to fight stress in a more constructive manner. Though we must all ride the STRESS EXPRESS at some time or another, we know how to get off at the next station rather than taking a world tour.

Subtle Boredom

How many of us slipped back because we weren't able to identify that we were being attacked by BOREDOM? Nothing is exciting forever—particularly the art of quitting smoking. The first few days we're kept from boredom by the very busy-ness of trying to get through withdrawal. Then we're so excited we made it that we aren't bored for a couple more weeks, or maybe months, or even years. And everyone initially pats us on the back and tells us to "hang in there," that we're courageous and all that; maybe we're even brought flowers or gifts—then one day the excitement is over. Everyone expects us "to be finished with quitting smoking" and "to get on with living." Then we are apt to get bored, or at least to have a letdown. And when we get bored, it is easy to forget just how hard it was to quit; our fantasies may turn to smoking "just one little cigarette" for a little excitement added to our lives.

So BEWARE OF BOREDOM. If you want excitement in your life, fantasize about withdrawal. You'll get excited remembering that YOU DON'T EVER WANT TO GO THROUGH WITHDRAWAL AGAIN—ONCE IS ENOUGH!!—IF YOU'VE DONE IT MANY TIMES, MAKE THIS YOUR LAST TIME! Take a couple of deep breaths and find something exciting to do that's positive!

Overconfidence That Borders on Cockiness

We need confidence in ourselves to quit smoking, but after we've made it for 10 days, or weeks, or months, we may get "puffed up" with cockiness. When we do this, a little man called the "humbling man" comes along and knocks us down. He doesn't do this only to ex-smokers, but to "perfect people" also. He follows me a lot; I know him well. The secret to avoiding his humbling lies in maintaining a balance between confidence and cockiness called "staying just plain grateful." The humbling man does not go after those who remain grateful—he has left me alone since I quit smoking six years ago—he knows I'm grateful.

If someone compliments you on making it, just say, "I'm so grateful that I've made it this far" or "I've been fortunate" or "I'm one of the lucky ones." These statements are a mixture of confidence and humbleness. They are not cocky statements, and the little humbling man will be kind to you. The balance between the two is very delicate—we not only end up successful ex-smokers, but accomplished "tightrope" walkers!

Denial of Addiction

Some people quit smoking easily—they were the ones who quit after the Surgeon General's report came out, in 1964. The rest of us were PERSISTENT, DEDICATED, and ADDICTED.

6

So often we went back to smoking because we thought we could fool around with "just one cigarette for old time's sake." And each time we learned that cigarettes will "fool around with our minds." We're dealing with nicotine—one of the most addictive and powerful known drugs—a chemical that is potent enough for use as an insecticide; a POISON used by natives on the ends of their spears to kill their prey immediately; and the chosen poison of an aborted assassin's plot during one of our nation's political scandals. Just because the tobacco industry is clever and devious enough to sell it to us in small, seemingly harmless doses through a "weapon" called cigarettes doesn't mean that it fails to do the assassin's job. We even PAY THEM MONEY to do it to us! Make a commitment to yourself to respect the potency of nicotine—and its dangers to our human system. If you do, you'll be more able to make the decision not to smoke in tempting situations. One of the people in my groups explained: "When someone offers me one, I say 'No THANKS—I'M AN ADDICT.'" She is strong—and she is a successful ex-smoker.

Fear of Success

Being able to quit smoking gives us such a feeling of success—why do we choose to give up that feeling? I don't know. Each of us is too individual to give one pat answer, but for some reason those of us who quit many times are willing to give up the success of quitting for the humiliation of returning to smoking. This phenomenon occurs with the giving up of ANY addiction, whether it be food, drugs, booze, or cigarettes. Maybe it's just that we've "practiced the addiction" longer than we've "practiced being without it." Maybe there are deep, psychological, Freudian reasons for it, but we don't have time to relive the past. It is gone. And none of us has a "tomorrow card," so we won't worry about what may happen tomorrow. ALL WE HAVE IS TODAY. Today is a good time to do the relaxation exercise. Repeat to yourself: "I am no longer trapped by the past; I am successful in quitting smoking and TODAY I am unwilling to be a smoker." Repeat this daily until your subconscious believes it and gets rid of the old destructive programs—or at least files them under "Lost." If you feel silly doing this because you are a logical, reasonable, analytical person, read the chapter on "Being a Fool," and ask yourself: "Where has my logic gotten me so far in regard to quitting smoking?" So learn to feel again, to believe in yourself again, and you really will be able to stay off cigarettes forever. You did not become a smoker without practice, so be willing to practice the art of not smoking. If you start to bombard your own success, take a minute to ask yourself, "Why don't I want success?" I don't have the answer for you—only YOU do!!

The Flashback Drawback

This flashback syndrome is only serious enough for about two out of 20 smokers to have to deal with, but it should be mentioned. Here is an example of how it may happen: Let's say that a man named John started smoking at age 16 when his best friend stole his girlfriend (rejection-pain #1), and, although the smoking didn't take away the emotional pain, it was like a temporary bandage that "soothed" it just a little. Then five years later he marries. He is happy and he stops smoking. Ten years later he gets divorced and starts smoking again (rejection-pain #2). He is now happily remarried and wants to stop smoking. He manages to quit but finds to his surprise that his thoughts are flashing back to a 16-year-old rejection from a girlfriend, to the pain of his divorce, and it all seems ridiculous but it still hurts! He can't tell anyone because they wouldn't understand, so he goes back to smoking.

Other incidents can flash back too, like the loss of a child, the loss of parents or of a mate. What is important is to realize that this is not reason enough to be going back to smoking. Get help! "The strong get help and the weak go about destroying their lives." If you want to help yourself without professional help, accept the pain. Get it out. Don't keep it inside. I've heard it said, "Ulcers are just TEARS turned INWARD." So, admit that the pain, rejection, or loss DO hurt; allow yourself to MOURN, give it time to HEAL, and then get on with your life! A friend who went through such flashbacks found she could only face her pain while standing in the shower. While there she could dredge it all up to her conscious thought; she would end up crying, but as the shower water washed down the drain, she was amazed to find that her pain did too. Slowly she was able to release her turmoil and eventually found herself "healed" for good.

When we no longer have cigarettes to "soothe" the pain or to help "deny" it, we need to learn to deal with stress situations or stressful thoughts in our own ways in order to be free of them once and for all. It feels so much better in the long run and doesn't leave us with unresolved burdens, even subconscious ones, to carry around.

> *Re confrontation: When you have been off cigarettes for awhile and you have either a personal or business confrontation and get the urge to smoke 'just one to get me through this'.*
> *Ask yourself: "Why would I have that first deadly cigarette because of someone who isn't even on my side?" —L. Bryson*

QUIT DAY

III
Preparation for Quit Day

"Life is what happens when we are making other plans"—Thomas
La Mance

The above quote says it well and can apply to the life experience called "quitting smoking." While you are planning a smooth quitting experience, LIFE will happen. So you need to prepare for life before you prepare for quitting smoking, and this means being realistic. Being realistic means understanding three basic or universal laws that affect all human beings.

Life Will Always Deal Out Stress in Some Form Or Another.

Does this mean that it is impossible to give up smoking? No. In fact if you can accept this premise, it will be much easier to give up smoking because you will be relieved of false expectations toward life. Then you can get on with the business of dealing with stress, and learning to relieve stress. You can reread the chapter on withdrawal and the chapter on stress management. You can learn the relaxation exercise before you quit smoking. You can have relaxation tapes on hand to play. You can write for a free booklet called "STRESS" that Blue Cross has designed.*

Some of the most relaxed and peaceful people I know have excess stress in their lives; they have just learned to FLOW with it rather than FIGHT it. They have learned to take a few minutes a day to learn to relax.

Life Is Sometimes Unfair

This is not meant to be a negative statement—it is a realistic statement. If we can accept the premise that life is sometimes unfair, then we don't expect too much of it! This, in turn, keeps us from being continually disappointed, and needing cigarettes to "soothe" the disappointment.

Success Does Not Come Magically

Life has been known to throw obstacles in the path of success. Since life does that, why not just "catch them" and turn them into challenges? Sometimes a challenge is just a blessing in disguise because it can "distract" you from the temporary misery of giving up smoking and give you something else to think about! Many ex-smokers say they might not have made it if life was so boring that all they had time to do was feel sorry for themselves without cigarettes. Since stress seems to come looking for us, let's be realistic enough to plan ahead and be READY for it.

In fact, so many of the smokers I've worked with recently have just lost a mate, are in the middle of a divorce or separation, or have other heavy stress in their lives, but they have become realistic enough to realize that if they sit around smoking and waiting for the stress to disappear, they will never stop smoking. They also realize that they don't need the "smoking problem" on

*Write or call, Blue Cross—Public Information

top of all the other problems they may have. They've learned to take obstacles and turn them into challenges. By quitting smoking, they will better their health, save money, and gain back control of their lives. All these benefits will help them cope better and more efficiently with the losses and stresses they already have.

Be forewarned that many obstacles will appear while you are planning to quit smoking; they often come disguised as "valid excuses NOT to quit." This is normal. I probably broke the world record for excuses the first 26 times I tried to quit. Then I finally realized that the excuses were just good old NICOTINE talking. NICOTINE had control of my body, my mind, and my soul. But I learned to "talk back" to that batallion of voices in my head that appeared with every withdrawal urge. I learned to talk back LOUDER and FASTER than they did. And I finally won! YOU can too!

Please start getting used to the idea that the only way to quit smoking is "Cold Turkey." Cutting down for long periods of time only prolongs the inevitable agony. Who needs added agony? It keeps you in a constant state of withdrawal which is not only physically tiring, but mentally frustrating as well. Please remember that less than one person out of a hundred can smoke just one cigarette a day—why go with odds of 99.5% against you? I can be contrary and stubborn at times, but I am not ignorant—I avoid odds like that! "Cutting down" is just our favorite excuse for going "warm chicken" instead of "cold turkey."

Planning a successful quitting plan requires many things. Although you've accepted that stress and obstacles will come your way unplanned, don't go out LOOKING for them. Pick a week that you don't have big stress situations already on the agenda. Don't quit the week you do your income tax return. Don't quit the week your last child leaves home. Don't quit the week you plan to potty train your two-year-old. Don't quit the week you have your dog or cat put to sleep. Don't quit the week your smoking relatives come to visit.

You need to feel good! Eat well and get lots of rest before you quit. Learn the relaxation exercise before you quit—start making that a new habit. Talk to your doctor about taking a daily "stress tab" vitamin B complex. You need the cooperation of family, co-workers, and friends. If you don't have anyone to support you, I highly recommend joining a support group, one that is sponsored by a local organization, a Seventh-Day Adventist 5-day plan, or a local hospital plan such as I conduct in our city. Now . . . let's lay out the plan in more detail:

1. **HAVE THE FIRST WEEK AS PROBLEM-FREE AS POSSIBLE.** Of course we can't eliminate all possible mishaps, but leave that week on your calendar free to do nothing but attend to the necessities of living. Try not to make appointments with people who cause you to feel stressful or uncomfortable. Try not to go places where you might be reminded of unpleasant situations. Make yourself as comfortable as possible. Spend some time reading the recommended books listed at the end of this book, so you can learn how to relax and to deal with stress more effectively.

Most important of all, avoid people with whom you smoke—if at all possible. If they are in your immediate family, ask them please not to smoke in front of you. This is an obvious courtesy, and I hope it does not need further explanation. If there is a smoker you lunch with or get together with over a glass of beer, tell them it would be too tempting to meet the first couple of weeks. Liquor relaxes one to the point that the "goblins" take control. Don't give them that chance. Try to stick to sugarless juices or soda water and gingerale the first week—you'll be walking a tightrope for awhile—don't pull your own net out from under yourself. This request about liquor is not a moral judgment. It is a request based on the experiences of many smokers who didn't make it because they got "too relaxed" to remember they were in the middle of quitting smoking. They woke up the next day and remembered, and had to start all over.

11

The first week you may feel very vulnerable, sensitive to criticism, and deprived, so treat yourself well. TAKE YOUR CIGARETTE MONEY FOR A WEEK OF SMOKING—BUY YOURSELF A SMALL GIFT. Plan to do some pleasurable things like go out to dinner. Sit in the non-smoking section and get the feel of a non-smoker. Or have your hair styled in celebration for having smoke-free hair. Or go to a movie you've been wanting to see. Or plan to take many warm bubble baths. Each person has something that is very relaxing to them; plan to do it. The only exception to relaxing is getting intoxicated. If you are serious about quitting smoking, you'll take me seriously. And don't feel guilty for spending the money. You're not spending it on cigarettes, so you'll have $30–$90 more a month to play with.

Start early telling yourself that "I AM AN EX-SMOKER." Keep repeating this as positive reinforcement of your choice to quit smoking. Sound like brain-washing? You bet! This is how brain-washing works—constant repetitions until the subconscious believes it. Use it for a positive cause—YOU! You had to brainwash yourself to start smoking, so use it to quit. Those of us who have made it think of ourselves as ex-smokers. If we told ourselves we were still smokers, chances are we would be. Be sure to read Maxwell Maltz's book on Psycho-cybernetics. He is a physician and explains this very well in his book. Also, read Dennis Jaffe's Healing From Within; includes relaxation techniques extraordinaire.

2. **YOU NEED TO BE FEELING WELL.** As I said before, we're walking a tightrope when going off cigarettes. You need everything in your favor to quit. Good health is in your favor. Please ask your physician if he will give you permission to take some sort of Stress Tab—which is a vitamin complex with all of the B complex vitamins. They are called the stress vitamins because they feed the nerves, besides acting in many other roles in the body. Being water soluble, they are not stored in the body but are passed daily through body elimination. Recent research shows that smokers already tend to be deficient in these vitamins as smoking interferes with their absorption and efficiency in the body. There are researchers and physicians who disagree but I don't have time to argue. I know that they have helped many smokers through the crisis period. Some say, "It's all in the head." So what! In one breath we're told that 80% of physical problems are "in our head" or psychological. When we do something simple that makes us feel better, we're told, "It's all in your head." And again I repeat, "So what!" IF OUR HEADS ARE CAUSING THE PROBLEMS, LET OUR HEADS UNDO THE PROBLEMS. All I'm asking is for every variable to be in your favor. Ask your physician or pharmacist for help.

3. **PLEASE PLAN TO EAT ONLY HEALTHY FOODS WHILE YOU ARE QUITTING.** "You are what you eat," so why would you want to eat junk and feel accordingly? You wouldn't put junk into your automobile gas tank and expect it to run smoothly and get you where you want to go. Why would you put junk into your body and expect it to get you where you're going? "Where you're going" is to the world of becoming an ex-smoker. Make it easier on yourself by following the simple recommendations I've suggested. Read the books on nutrition in the Recommended Reading. They'll help. And they're really simple if you maintain an open and positive mind.

4. **DRINK LOTS OF WATER AND SUGARLESS JUICES.** They'll fill up your stomach and they are low-calorie. They also flush the nicotine more quickly from your body. The nicotine stays in your system for approximately two to three days. The sooner you get it out, the better. I talk about staying away from white sugar products because the B vitamins are necessary to metabolize carbohydrates, but YOU need them to maintain sanity—don't distract them away from that task. Besides, you get all the natural sugar you need in fresh fruits, whole grains, and complex

carbohydrates. The nutrition books will help you understand the difference between simple and complex carbohydrates. Try to eat fresh fruits, vegetables, eggs, low-fat meats such as poultry and fish, whole wheat grains and breads. <u>Stay away from white sugar and white flour.</u> Your body does not need to be busy processing junk. <u>Save</u> the energy to develop the stamina to stay off cigarettes.

5. **STOCK UP ON SUBSTITUTES AHEAD OF TIME.** Stock up on sugarless mints and gums. I think the exception to the sugar rule is lemon drops and suckers. They both take a <u>long time</u> to devour so you won't put away too many of them. They really seem to help some people, so use them if they sound appealing. The suckers keep both your hands and mouth busy, and this is helpful for people who need to keep their hands and mouths <u>occupied</u> when not smoking. Though I was a stress smoker primarily, I also like to keep my hands and mouth busy. I always carry sugarless mints with me. Some people like to keep a glass of <u>cold water</u> by their chair or on their desk at work. Maybe it only serves as a distraction, but that's what we're looking for—lots of distractions to keep your mind off cigarettes. Remember that from 10 to 60 times a day you've been reaching for a cigarette! You'll still keep reaching, but something else will have to be in its place.

6. **STOCK UP ON PLASTIC STRAWS.** Cut them in <u>half</u> so they are about the same length as a cigarette and "puff" on them.* The body feels relaxed and comfortable with this puffing sensation—it also takes in oxygen at about the same pace as smoking, so your subconscious is temporarily distracted. If someone asks you what you're doing, tell them you're "smoking a straw." <u>Try toothpicks. Try keeping a miniature box of raisins handy.</u>

7. **LEARN TO TAKE THREE DEEP BREATHS.** Do this whenever you get the urge for a smoke. It gets more oxygen to the brain. This is not only relaxing, but allows you to think more clearly and make the decision not to smoke that first cigarette. Remember, what you're fighting is that "first" cigarette. All it takes is one to start all over again. <u>The urge will be over in one to three minutes.</u>

For those who really need something in your hands to replace the cigarette, try playing with a lump of clay or Play Dough. Or roll marbles in your hand. Or knit or crochet. If you don't know how, you'll have the money you used to pay out for cigarettes to sign up for a class to learn.

There will always be people who give you a bad time for needing so many substitutes. Maybe they are "perfect people" who quit easily. Don't let them put you down. It's your mind, your body, and your choice, so accomplish your goal your way!

Take care of yourself and get in good condition before you quit. We have only <u>one</u> body—we don't get refills, so treat it with respect. So many people treat their bodies badly and wonder why they go through life on slow speed and reverse. They take <u>better</u> care of their automobiles. Or their pets. Or their golf clubs. Or their surf boards.

8. **YOU NEED THE COOPERATION OF FAMILY, FRIENDS, CO-WORKERS.** Chapter XI discusses this in more detail, so run off copies of the chapter and pass it out to friends, family, and co-workers. If you work in an office, you can put a sign on your desk that says, <u>Handle with care—I'm trying to give up smoking.</u>" Or devise your own appropriate sign. You might ask your boss to be a little tolerant for a week or so—remind him your change in disposition is only temporary. Remind your mate not to take you at face value when you become unreasonable, difficult, or spout off obscenities. Or if you cry for no apparent reason.

*For obvious reasons, recovering cocaine users would not be advised to use straws as "substitutes" . . . "puffing" on an empty Aqua Filter would be more suitable.

Tell your smoking co-workers that you'll have to avoid the cigarette breaks for awhile—it's too easy to follow them around trying to <u>inhale</u> when they <u>exhale</u>. They'll understand if you put it that way. The only attitude they won't understand is self-righteousness. Plan to be around people who don't smoke. This takes making changes. Be sure to read the chapter on making changes. Your life will be changed—but for the better.

9. **START FIGURING OUT WHY AND WHEN YOU SMOKE.** Each of us must make a personal analysis of WHY we smoke. No two smokers smoke alike. We can divide the categories into STRESS smoking, HABIT smoking, CRUTCH smoking, RELAXATION smoking, and STIMULATION AND HANDLING smoking. Since no two habit smokers smoke alike any more than two relaxation smokers smoke alike, there is a way of finding out what kind of smoker you are. Take the **Smoker's Test** (p. 15). This will help you prepare your "battle plan" so you come out on the winning side. Circle your three (3) highest scores. Then read about **Smoking Types** (p. 16) which gives tips and suggestions for each type of smoker to make it easier to quit.

Wrap your cigarette pack in the **Wrap Sheet** (p. 17). When you get the urge for a cigarette, take out the pack, unwrap it and write down how you are feeling at the time. Then use the **Urgency Table** (p. 18) to determine the urgency or need rating. You'll find out that most of your cigarettes are just habit. There will be some that you will feel fairly uncomfortable without, and there will be your "favorite cigarettes" which get the highest urgency and need rating. By breaking it down this way, you can then accept that your favorite cigarettes are the ones that will give you the <u>most</u> trouble when you don't have them.

10. **BEGIN TO PRACTICE WELLNESS TECHNIQUES THAT "MIMIC" THE ACTION OF NICOTINE IN YOUR SYSTEM.** No wonder that we get so addicted to nicotine—it is one of the few drugs that gives us both a "stimulant" effect and a "depressant" effect. We get a 7–10 second "hit" to the brain as nicotine acts on the heart, blood vessels, digestive tract, and kidneys. After the initial stimulant effect, the drug then "depresses" activity of parts of the brain and nervous system. We become "anesthetized"—of course we feel relaxed! Unfortunately, the drug <u>cannot solve</u> our stress/anxiety problems—it just causes us to "postpone" thinking about them—OR SOLVING THEM WITH POSITIVE ACTION!

Moderate exercise or walking can "mimic" the stimulation/depressant effect. We are <u>stimulated</u> by the exercise—then a <u>relaxation</u> phase will occur. <u>Cold water</u> gives a <u>stimulation</u> effect. Some researchers feel sunflower seeds give a <u>stimulation</u> (push the "adrenalin" button)—then give <u>relaxation</u> (contain calming oils and B vitamins). Deep breathing, relaxation, centering, prayer, massage, sauna, warm bath, "attitude of gratitude" mimic the <u>relaxation</u> effect.

THERE <u>ARE</u> ALTERNATIVES TO NICOTINE—ENJOY THEM!

Why do you smoke?

Here are some statements made by people to describe what they get out of smoking cigarettes. How often do you feel this way when smoking?

Circle one number for each statement. Important: ANSWER EVERY QUESTION.

	always	fre-quently	occa-sionally	seldom	never
A. I smoke cigarettes in order to keep myself from slowing down.	5	4	3	2	1
B. Handling a cigarette is part of the enjoyment of smoking it.	5	4	3	2	1
C. Smoking cigarettes is pleasant and relaxing.	5	4	3	2	1
D. I light up a cigarette when I feel angry about something.	5	4	3	2	1
E. When I have run out of cigarettes I find it almost unbearable until I can get them.	5	4	3	2	1
F. I smoke cigarettes automatically without even being aware of it.	5	4	3	2	1
G. I smoke cigarettes to stimulate me, to perk myself up.	5	4	3	2	1
H. Part of the enjoyment of smoking a cigarette comes from the steps I take to light up.	5	4	3	2	1
I. I find cigarettes pleasurable.	5	4	3	2	1
J. When I feel uncomfortable or upset about something, I light up a cigarette.	5	4	3	2	1
K. I am very much aware of the fact when I am not smoking a cigarette.	5	4	3	2	1
L. I light up a cigarette without realizing I still have one burning in the ashtray.	5	4	3	2	1
M. I smoke cigarettes to give me a "lift."	5	4	3	2	1
N. When I smoke a cigarette, part of the enjoyment is watching the smoke as I exhale it.	5	4	3	2	1
O. I want a cigarette most when I am comfortable and relaxed.	5	4	3	2	1
P. When I feel "blue" or want to take my mind off cares and worries, I smoke cigarettes.	5	4	3	2	1
Q. I get a real gnawing hunger for a cigarette when I haven't smoked for a while.	5	4	3	2	1
R. I've found a cigarette in my mouth and didn't remember putting it there.	5	4	3	2	1

This is Test III of the Smoker's Self-Testing Kit developed by Daniel H. Horn, PhD. and originally printed by the National Clearinghouse for Smoking and Health, DHEW.

U.S. DEPARTMENT OF HEALTH, EDUCATION, AND WELFARE
Public Health Service
National Institutes of Health

DHEW Publication No. (NIH) 79-1822

How to score

1. Enter the number you have circled for each question in the spaces below, putting the number you have circled to Question A over line A, to Question B over line B, etc.

A _____ + G _____ + M _____ = _____
Stimulation

B _____ + H _____ + N _____ = _____
Handling

C _____ + I _____ + O _____ = _____
Pleasurable Relaxation

D _____ + J _____ + P _____ = _____
Crutch: Tension Reduction

E _____ + K _____ + Q _____ = _____
Craving: Psychological Addiction

F _____ + L _____ + R _____ = _____
Habit

2. Add the 3 scores on each line to get your totals. For example, the sum of your scores over lines A, G, and M gives you your score on Stimulation—lines B, H, and N give the score on Handling, etc.

Totals

Scores can vary from 3 to 15. Any score 11 and above is high; any score 7 and below is low.

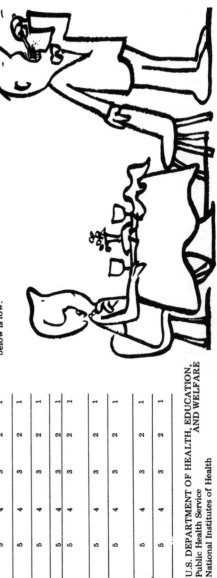

STIMULATION

These cigarettes give you an "up" feeling and get you going, even pull you out of bed in the morning. So try . . . a brisk walk or running in place · chewing gum · a new stimulating hobby · a <u>cold</u> glass of water or juice · chewing ice cubes.

HANDLING

You need these to keep the "fidgets" away. So try . . . doodling · cutting a straw in half and holding it like a cigarette · handling "worry" beads or a smooth stone · playing with "pop" beads · playing with a plastic cigarette or toothpick or pencil or pen · taking up knitting or crocheting or needlework.

RELAXATION or "REWARD"

These are the pleasurable times of day or night when you want to sit back and relax or reward yourself for jobs or chores well done. So try . . . thinking back to what you used for rewards and relaxation <u>before</u> you started smoking · substituting another pleasurable substitute such as low-cal, healthy foods · social activity that you enjoy · hiring a reputable massage therapist to give you a weekly back rub · buying yourself a trinket or piece of clothing you have admired · best of all, reading some of the recommended reading in back of this book and learning some good stress management techniques such as daily relaxation—you are worth it!!

HABIT

These are the cigarettes that help you answer the telephone, start the car, prepare the meals, write out the bills, drink your coffee, get you through endless paperwork and amount to HABIT and REPETITION. So try . . . becoming <u>aware</u> of each of these habit cigarettes (the wrap sheet on page 17 helps determine these also). Ask yourself, "Do I really <u>need</u> this cigarette?" and have an alternative plan.

CRUTCH or STRESS

I find these are just cigarettes that we have used to get us through stress situations. You can get through the situations without them and be immensely rewarded with self-pride. Read the stress management chapter. Start reading books on stress management. Attend local stress workshops.

CRAVING or ADDICTION

Craving is just having cigarettes on our mind every waking moment and even craving them in the middle of the night. Just <u>admitting</u> that we are addicted eliminates the control they have over us; resisting the temptation to go back to smoking is usually easy because we <u>never</u> want to go through quitting again. Addicts cannot "taper off" . . . cold turkey is the only way!!

Cigarette Wrap Sheet

DIRECTIONS: Please do this exercise for <u>one</u> day. In the morning, wrap your cigarette pack in this sheet as if you were wrapping a present. Each time you feel the urge for a cigarette, unwrap the pack and rate your "urgency need" defined by the Urgency Table on the following page. Also record where you are, whether you are alone or with other people, and whether you smoked the cigarette or not. Even if you decide <u>not</u> to have the cigarette after all, please still record it.

CIGARETTE #	WHERE ARE YOU?	ARE YOU ALONE?	URGENCY NEED	SMOKED CIGARETTE	DID NOT SMOKE
1					
2					
3					
4					
5					
6					
7					
8					
9					
10					
11					
12					
13					
14					
15					
16					
17					
18					
19					
20					
21					
22					
23					
24					
25					
26					
27					
28					
29					
30					
31					
32					
33					
34					
35					
36					
37					
38					
39					
40					

• • • Urgency Table • • •

#1 *URGENCY—Favorite Cigarettes*

These are the cigarettes you'll miss the most. You'd tell a lie to anyone, including yourself, to get at this one. You would walk a mile in a snowstorm for this one. If you got to your destination and there were no cigarettes, you'd settle for an "old butt." And it would even taste good. You wouldn't care if you have to borrow the "old butt." These are the cigarettes that work with the "goblins" in your head. They are both employees of Big Boss Nicotine. Probably 4 to 5 cigarettes per day are of this intense craving.

These cigarettes and the needs associated with them are the ones that will pop up in your head months and years later, such as when you have a fight with your mate, boss, or children. You'll have just one of these "favorites" to "show them." But all we do is show ourselves that Nicotine wins again. Plan to eradicate them successfully.

#2 *URGENCY—The Oh-Well-Might-As-Well*

These will not be nearly as demanding as your "favorite" cigarettes. You wouldn't walk a mile for it, but you might venture around the block for one on a sunny day. You wouldn't lie or steal for one, but you'd take one if it was offered to you. The urge is not panic, just desire. Probably about 5 to 10 cigarettes a day are of this nature.

#3 *URGENCY—Just for the Habit of It*

These are the easiest to beat. They are just pure habit—like eating, or sleeping. By the time you unwrap your pack and start to analyze the need, you'll forget why you were wanting one. These habit cigarettes, fortunately, constitute the largest part of your smoking habit.

THINGS I <u>LIKE</u> ABOUT SMOKING	THINGS I <u>DON'T</u> LIKE ABOUT SMOKING

BEFORE you quit smoking, start listing your LIKES and DISLIKES of smoking . . . keep <u>adding on</u> to the DISLIKE list after you quit. AFTER you quit smoking, cut this sheet in half and <u>keep only the DISLIKE list</u>. Post it so that you can remind yourself that you really wanted to quit smoking when you find it hard to remember WHY you started all this in the first place!!

So—this is where you start preparing your battle plan. Whenever you have the urge for your favorite cigarette, you'll need to have planned beforehand something else to take its place. These favorite cigarettes are the ones that have been friends with the "goblins" in your head. They've been working together very well to keep you addicted. Your battle plan has to be better than theirs.

10. **BY UNWRAPPING THE CIGARETTE PACK, YOU GAIN STILL ANOTHER INSIGHT.** You'll find that by the time you unwrap them and write down the urgency need, the desire will disappear. You'll know that these are just habit smokes. You really don't need them, but as long as they're there, you'll smoke them.

For some people their very favorite cigarette will be the FIRST-OF-THE-MORNING SMOKE. For someone else it will be one AFTER THEIR DINNER MEAL. Or the one with their MORNING COFFEE. Or the one they have ON THE WAY TO WORK IN THE CAR. Let's say that it is the first-of-the-morning one that actually has the power to drag you out of bed. When you quit and find you can't look forward to it, you may find yourself glued to the sheets. So what are you going to do instead? YOU NEED TO FIND ANOTHER STIMULUS. Some people have a glass of ICE WATER brought to them. This is the kind of service that your children would like to do for you—they'll feel they're helping you to quit. Or you can get up and take a cold shower. Most just take a WARM SHOWER. But some people who have made it had to use the COLD SHOWER. Or you may just have to have someone actually pull you out of bed. The important point is, have it planned ahead because when you wake up and you're drowsy, and you know your favorite cigarette is waiting for you, it's easy to let the "goblins" talk you into having one. You're too vulnerable when you're sleepy.

Say that your favorite one is the one in the car. You're actually conditioned to the point of believing that your car won't start or drive unless you light up. This is a hard one to break. You'll have to fill the ashtray with something besides cigarette butts—try sugarless mints, gum, or straws. Some people have had to remove the ashtray completely for the first few weeks. Or you might have a box of toothpicks handy to put in your mouth. Then see if the car still starts. Mine did.

There are some people who don't even have a "favorite" cigarette. They don't really like the taste of tobacco. They don't even like their smoking habit. They just happened to "do it for fun" long enough that they woke up one morning addicted to the smoking habit. So they just light up at every change of pace. They are pure HABIT or ADDICTION smokers; they still have to go "cold turkey" like the rest of us.

If you find out you are a STRESS smoker, you'll have to learn other ways of dealing with a stress. Identify your stress, and get it out in the open. I had been a stress smoker. I had always been a "people pleaser." I was cool and collected most of the time. Then I stopped smoking. For a while I thought I was the "original split-personality kid." I became "icky." I still wanted to be loved even though I was acting "icky," but people weren't too impressed with my lack of cool. I blamed it on "not being myself." Then who was I? After being able to accept that I had all those feelings inside, it became O.K. They started cooling down, and I started dealing with them.

THE ONE RULE TO THIS IS: ALWAYS BE HONEST WITH YOURSELF. So you have an undesirable characteristic that was hiding behind your smoking habit? Let it out—deal with it—and it will be O.K. If it doesn't seem to be O.K. within a reasonable amount of time, get help for it. So what if you'd rather keep those emotions "under control" and "boiling inside"? They'll boil all right, and when they finally boil over, they become an ulcer or a heart attack, or a breakdown. Let them out, and they'll be content to stay on "simmer." We can deal with "simmer."

11. **I'LL EMPHASIZE AGAIN—IF THE PROBLEMS ARE TOO BIG, GET HELP.** It takes strength to ask for help. The strong do—then they get on with their lives. The weak don't—they just stop living. Of course, some of you won't have any of these problems. I'm just throwing some reactions out, so if you happen to have them, you'll know you're not crazy. You didn't "invent" these emotions—they were given to the first people on earth when they were created and given brains.

Yes—I have really learned the art of TALKING TO MYSELF since I quit smoking. And getting to know myself. And liking myself. AND ACCEPTING MYSELF. You'll really find yourself enjoying your own company more when you stop smoking. You've removed the "CIGARETTE PLUG." You may surprise yourself and others at first, though. One of the women in my group called herself "Cool Helen" before she quit smoking. She said she became a "little magpie" after she quit. At first her husband wasn't sure he liked her constant conversation, but he supported her and is glad he did. He has a healthy, communicative wife now. She's proud of what she's done, and she said their marriage became much stronger.

If you want to quit smoking but feel you need to continue because of social pressure, you really need to learn to talk to yourself about what is important in your life? Is it what others think of you? Or is it your own health and self-esteem? It can be more difficult when your family members, co-workers, and everyone around you seem to smoke. But if you look hard enough, you can find someone who doesn't smoke regardless of the social pressure, and ask them how they do it. Try to spend more time with people who don't smoke. This is only necessary for the first few weeks that you are becoming confortable as a non-smoker. The first few days off cigarettes the exhaled smoke from smokers can actually smell tempting and good—you may feel inclined to follow them around. After awhile, your nonsmoking instincts will take over—this is self-preservation, and you'll no longer find cigarette smoke smelling good.

Many of your cigarettes may be your "favorite" ones because they are associated with friends and good times. You'll have to make some new good times. Try running—going to movies—rediscovering the library—anything that feels good and is good for you. Or you can convince the smokers around you to quit with you.

START TELLING YOURSELF, "I AM STRONG AND I AM AN EX-SMOKER." Repeat this only in the present tense, "I am." If your subconscious hears it in the future tense, it will stay in the future tense and never happen. You can resist the pressure; decide to do it now. And perhaps those around you will be so impressed they may join you. Use the same peer pressure that got you to start smoking to stop your smoking. This is why stop-smoking groups work so well. Everyone is encouraging everyone else to make it! It is positive peer pressure.

12. **TRY YOUR OWN AVERSION TECHNIQUE.** Even though I really don't believe in using a lot of aversion therapy, there is one aversion technique I can highly recommend as it worked for me. The reason I don't use aversion therapy extensively is because it is a negative input. You smoke until you become repulsed or sick and then supposedly you'll never want another cigarette. For many it works, but I decided if it worked for me, I'd then need to see a counselor to find out why I enjoyed "pain and revulsion" so much!

HERE IS THE TECHNIQUE I USED. I needed to mentally picture my cigarettes in a very disgusting position so that every time I got an urge, that mental picture would flash up front and wipe out the urge for a cigarette. So I imagined that my cigarette pack was lying out in the middle of a freeway near our home. Then a nutria comes waddling along and sniffs at my cigarettes on the freeway. (A nutria is a river mammal that appears to be to be a mixture of mole, rat, weasel, and armadillo; they are always lying squished on our highways around here.) I visualized the nutria being hit by a car and "squishing" all over my pack of cigarettes. I kept telling myself that my cigarettes would taste like that if I had one. And who wants to smoke something with a "nutria" flavor? I repeated this visual picture many times in order for it to be able to flash up front immediately. And I still imagine my cigarettes that way. Every time I pass a nutria waddling across the road, I treat them with respect. I stop for them—they helped me to stop smoking. People in my groups have come up with some really "icky" mental pictures that have worked for them.

This is the only aversion I recommend. The most important thing is that you learn "HOW" and "WHY" and "WHEN" you smoke and, if you are willing to take the time and energy to find out, you'll have changed your thinking process in a permanent and positive fashion. You'll begin to really know yourself, and then you won't have to smoke anyway.

13. **SOME PEOPLE NEED TO MAKE A RITUAL OF QUITTING.** One man just took his last pack of cigarettes outside and "killed" them—he hammered them to death. Some keep their last pack on a shelf or mantel or in a drawer as a trophy of sorts—a reminder of who is in control. Most of us cannot be tempted that way, but for some it works. Another person may want to "drown" their last pack of cigarettes. Maybe you'll want to embalm your last pack in liquid plastic and use it for a paper weight. My way of letting my cigarette habit go forever was to write the farewell song, "Paper Lady Blues." Do what works for YOU.

Many people have expressed to me that they can't imagine giving up cigarettes forever, so they tell themselves that they are POSTPONING the next cigarette for a day, a month, or even 10 years. And they take it a day, or a month, or a year at a time. Their psyche can take the postponement. When asked if they quit smoking, they say, "I'm postponing my smoking." For them it works.

The moral to this chapter is that "THOSE WHO PLAN AHEAD, GET AHEAD." So write down your plan and strategy to make it through the first day, then the second, then the second week. Take it a day at a time. If you can make it through the first day, you can make it through the second, and so on. Continue doing this until the act of not smoking starts to feel as comfortable as the act of smoking once did. Smoking will then become just a memory rather than a reality. You will start feeling less and less deprived. You'll start to feel joyous and grateful. Start thinking of yourself now as free from smoking. Keep repeating, "I am an ex-smoker!" If things become too unbearable, just let yourself CRY—I heard a small child say, "Crying lets the bad feelings out, and the good feelings in."

Just when all logic
had failed me,
I climbed on a rainbow
And hope—
Became my reality

scripsit gmcastor 1983

23

Psychological and Physiological Responses to Nicotine Withdrawal

Negative Responses

Depression
Confusion
Anxiety
Awareness of lack of coping skills
Irritability
Increased anger response
Increased jaw tension and teeth-clenching
Insomnia/sleepiness
Diarrhea/constipation
Restlessness
Dullness
"Grief or mourning" response/loss response
Increased tendency to cry
Impairment of concentration
Impairment of memory (short-term)
Dizziness
Skin irritation/rashes
Sensation behind eyes
Weight gain
Nausea
Water retention
Gastro-intestinal symptoms, flatulence

Positive Responses

Decrease in heart rate
Decrease in blood pressure
Increase in extremity temperature
Slower rhythms in the EEG
Increased REM sleep
Increase in smell and taste
Increased blood flow to brain
Decrease in free fatty acids
Decrease in carboxyhemoglobin
Increased cilia response
Decrease in excess adrenalin output
Increased respiratory functions
Increase in self-esteem

Sources

Behavioral Medicine—Changing Health Lifestyles. Davidson, Park O., Ph.D. and Davidson, Sheena M., M.S.N. New York: Brunner/Mazel Publishers, 1980.

Merck Manual. 13th edition. Merck, Sharp & Dohme Research Laboratories. Rahway, New Jersey, 1977.

Addictions—Issues & Answers. Jaffe, Jerome, M. D., Petersen, Robert, Ph.D. Hodgson, Ray, Ph.D. Professor of Psychiatry, College of Physicians & Surgeons. Columbia University. New York, London: Harper & Row Publishers, 1980.

The Journal of Respiratory Diseases. Roger Bone, M.D., James Phillips, M.D. and Parimal Chowdhury, Ph.D. May, 1981, pp. 10–15.

IV
Actual Withdrawal from Nicotine

"Sometimes I go about pitying myself, and all the time I am being carried on great winds across the sky."—Chippewa Indian

This chapter title has been staring at me from the typewriter for four weeks. I just figured out why I kept postponing writing on nicotine withdrawal. My thinking had regressed to ancient medical psychology where the patients were told, "It won't hurt a bit." Then after the terrible pain had subsided, the patients wondered why they had been treated as simple fools. The tendency was there for me to tell you that nicotine withdrawal "won't hurt a bit, or at most only for a few minutes." But you are intelligent human beings and here is the reality.

Many people who are withdrawing from nicotine go through a week of hell before "sanity" returns. There are many ex-smokers who quit long ago who will state they suffered no pain, and determination is all it takes. To that I reply, "Congratulations! But I maintain that those who quit easily had already quit. We're dealing with hard-core smokers!"

What really happens to smokers is that the body takes months to adjust to the onslaught of nicotine circulating through the bloodstream. The body will certainly rebel when the nicotine leaves the bloodstream. You may wonder if the pain is worth it. Believe me, it is! You can afford one week of misery out of your lifetime to save your life. What is ONE WEEK of misery compared to the YEARS of misery that emphysema and cancer patients suffer? If you doubt me, request a visit through the emphysema or cancer ward nearest you. You'll not treasure this visit, but at least it will put the few miserable days you'll encounter in to perspective. Give the gift of freedom to yourself.

1. **REMEMBER TO PLAN ON TREATING YOURSELF VERY WELL THE FIRST WEEK.** Actually, most experts agree that nicotine will leave your body within three days. This constitutes the end of the physical battle with nicotine. what you have left is the psychological battle of fighting the habit of lighting up thirty to sixty times a day that we began discussing in Chapter II. What are you going to do instead? Of all the cigarettes you smoke, you will find that five to ten of them are your favorite and necessary ones. The rest are mainly habit and easier to replace. It is your favorite ones you need to be concerned about. Find something new to put in their place.

2. **SET YOURSELF UP FOR SUCCESS.** Practice some of the techniques from the suggested readings in the chapter on weight control. These techniques are universal and can be applied to break any addiction or change any habit.

PUTTING SOMETHING IN PLACE of your favorite cigarettes brings up the next effect that ex-smokers may suffer from. This is a feeling of emptiness which is very hard to describe. Some ex-smokers define it as the feeling of having a big black empty hole in the core of their being. Other ex-smokers compare it to the loss of a dear friend or relative. Some compare it to the empty feeling that divorce brings. What is really important is that a loss is being felt. Your cigarettes have been psychological friends to you for a long time. They do not nag, quarrel, or judge you. They are just there if you need them. Whenever we suffer a loss, we need to mourn. Then we need to start adjusting.

3. **FIRST WE NEED TO PUT SOMETHING IN THE PLACE OF CIGARETTES.** If you aren't willing to make this replacement, you will be one of those ex-smokers who feels life is no longer worth living. The best replacement you can give yourself is to do something you've always wanted to do. You'll have many extra dollars a month to do these things. Or start volunteering your services to many of the worthwhile service or volunteer organizations. Stop thinking only about yourself and your cigarettes. There is a saying that, "The smallest package in the world is someone all wrapped up in themselves." Any of us who are successful ex-smokers have had to adopt a positive attitude. Then the attitude becomes a habit, because we practice it as faithfully as we practiced our smoking.

4. **EACH SMOKER IS UNIQUE.** Every smoker has an individual chemical makeup and some of you will experience feelings, sensations, and emotions that I am not discussing. It is an excellent way to learn about yourself if you are able to stand back, be patient, and then try to deal objectively with these emotions. Again, if you are not able to do this by yourself, seek professional help. You may feel "crazy" at times, or disoriented, or lightheaded. You are not crazy. You are experiencing nicotine withdrawal. When it seems the very worst, ask yourself if you ever want something this cruel and powerful controlling your life again. I mean, ask yourself out loud.

5. **THE MOTTO FOR THIS MAIN EVENT IS: "THE SMOKER WHO TALKS TO HIMSELF IS MASTER OF NICOTINE."** You must learn to talk convincingly to yourself. NICOTINE will get the anti-forces in your head talking so loudly, you'll be outshouted if you don't learn this technique. All successful people and all winners talk to themselves. They talk about success and winning. If this seems too foolish, you're already talking like a loser. It is your choice to be a winner.

Whenever the anti-forces in my head start shouting negative ideas to me, I remember the childhood story of The Little Engine That Could. It is about a little engine who starts up a steep mountain chanting to himself, "I think I can, I think I can, I think I can." Then as he nears the top, he starts chanting, "I know I can, I know I can, I know I can." As he goes over the top of the mountain and starts downhill, he chants, "I knew I could, I knew I could, I knew I could." It's a simple story, but success is always simple. YOU decide . . . either you can or you can't. Then the work of maintaining the success begins. Just when you think you can't make it through another day without cigarettes, you'll be nearing the top of the mountain. Hang in there, all the time talking success to yourself, and soon you'll be going down the other side of the mountain of success. And it's downhill the rest of the way.

If you are willing to read Psycho-Cybernetics and Healing From Within (see the suggested reading list), you will begin to understand the power that you have over your own thinking process. You will begin to accept the fact that you have a choice in how you REACT to situations. These books bring home the fact that if you repeat a thought process to yourself long enough, it will become a permanent program in your computer—until you decide to change it. One example of the power of suggestion is that many times I tried to quit smoking from age sixteen to twenty. Back then we didn't know all the details and pain of withdrawal because none of our peers were quitting and experiencing withdrawal and we weren't about to go to the library and read about it. The point I'm trying to make is that because I was not programmed to believe in nicotine withdrawal, I did not experience it. I only started smoking again because of peer pressure, not because I was having a nicotine fit. Only years later when "nicotine fits" were the big topic of discussion among smokers trying to quit did I accept it as a part of quitting, and from then on I experienced severe nicotine withdrawal every time I quit thereafter.

For some people the fear of quitting is worse than the actual pain of withdrawal. For them it's all downhill once the decision is made. The decision-making process was their greatest hurdle.

6. **YOU MAY FEEL TEMPORARILY DEPRESSED AND LETHARGIC.** I call this the "slug syndrome." Your body has been on a constant "upper" or stimulant with nicotine. You are now coming down to the world of an ex-smoker. Not only is there a physical chemical change in your body, but an emotional change. You have always had the "reward" of a cigarette for getting a task or job done. You could always light up when you're through. Now you will miss that reward. It will take time to learn to do the task because it needs to be done rather than because there is a "cigarette at the end of the rainbow," so to speak. Give yourself that time to adjust. Read the suggested books for help on reprogramming yourself.

7. **SOME PEOPLE DON'T LIKE THE LIGHTHEADEDNESS THEY FEEL.** Some will feel very hyperactive rather than lethargic. Can you think back and remember how you felt after that very first cigarette? Did you feel very high, dizzy, and hyperactive? Or just sick? Although your body became adjusted to that high feeling, the body was not meant to run with the gas pedal pushed clear to the floor. If you are feeling very hyperactive and light-headed, then you would benefit from doing the relaxation exercises in the Suggested Reading. Keep repeating to yourself, "I am an ex-smoker." Be sure to repeat it only in the present tense. You don't want your subconscious taking it as a future order, but as a present order. Every time you lit a cigarette in the past, you were internally saying to yourself, "I am a smoker." If you were a two-pack-a-day smoker, as I was, you reaffirmed this belief approximately 21,840 times a year. So you can see why you need to put a lot of effort into reaffirming your belief in yourself as an ex-smoker.

You may think that you are having more "bad days" without your cigarettes. THIS IS NOT TRUE. Non-smokers and ex-smokers also have bad days. Life just doesn't deal out all good days to anyone. Just as we enjoy good days, we can learn to benefit from bad days. I'm sorry it took me the first thirty years of my life to learn this valuable lesson. I used to fight bad days by either pretending there wasn't a problem, or I would scrub floors in hopes the problems would disappear with the dirt. Then I realized that bad days were friends in disguise. Now I flow with them, rather than fight them. They are my personal signal to slow down, to re-evaluate my present thinking pattern. They give me a chance to be with myself and ask myself if I'm growing and learning or just riding in a rut.

I no longer pretend that I'm not having a bad day; I no longer try to scrub problems away. I get into low gear and try to do something for someone else. Maybe it's just calling or writing a friend. I push myself out of my procrastination and give a little extra to someone else. There are the little things we manage to avoid while we're in high gear. Then the greatest thing happens: GOOD DAYS FOLLOW, and I can go back to high gear with a feeling of accomplishment and renewal. Again this is a time for internal talk. I say, "O.K., Linda, so it's a bad day. What are you going to do about it?" When I suggest doing things for other people, I am serious. Some people call volunteers "do-gooders."

Again, you have a choice in the matter. You can "do bad" and feel accordingly, or you can "do good" and feel accordingly. And when you feel good, you won't feel like smoking cigarettes. You'll have that self-respect that leads to self-control. So, on your bad days, one thing you can do is get out of yourself and into someone else's life. You'll still continue to have bad days, but remember . . . it is not because you don't have a cigarette. It will be because you are growing and changing. Make it a positive experience.

8. **WHEN THE URGE FOR A CIGARETTE HITS, REMEMBER THAT IT WILL BE OVER IN 2–3 MINUTES.** So take your three deep breaths. Take them slowly. This gets more oxygen to the brain which not only relaxes you but enables you to think more clearly and to make your decision not to smoke. After the three minutes are up, you'll be relieved that you didn't have that cigarette. And you will be refreshed to fight the next urge. It could be compared to labor pains. You know there will be another one, but eventually the pain stops, and there is a beautiful reward. Your reward for not smoking will be renewed self-respect. After the first few days, the urges will be much less frequent and less intense. They'll continue diminishing until they become only "twinges."

I've been asked if I still ever want cigarettes. Of course I still get twinges for them, but I also get twinges for chocolate cake, Burt Reynolds, and licorice, which I cannot have. These are just twinges, not urges filled with panic as in the first few days of withdrawal. How could I totally forget cigarettes after having lit approximately 327,699 of them in my smoking career? They became a part of me. They became me. But I chose to let them go and put them into the back of my computer. They are now filed under "M" for "Memories." When I go to sleep, sometimes my subconscious takes over and lets the "Memories" out to play and I have a dream about smoking. It's great to wake up after a smoking dream and realize that it was just a fantasy. It was fun and no one was hurt in the process.

9. **THERE WILL ALWAYS BE PEOPLE WHO CHOOSE TO BE MISERABLE FOR YEARS AFTER THEY QUIT SMOKING.** They say their life was over when they quit smoking. They thrive in their misery because it feels so good. Please try to avoid such people when you are trying to quit. They cannot be of any help to you. They are self-appointed martyrs who refused to fill their emptiness with something positive. Actually, my opinion is that these people are still smoking. They don't light up, but their habit is still with them in their hearts, and it makes them miserable. Eventually you have to let the habit go completely. When I wrote Paper Lady Blues, I realized that it was my final parting song to a habit that I had enjoyed for a long time. ALLOW YOURSELF TEARS—AND MOURNING—THEN SAY "SO LONG!"

Quite a few people have mentioned that they feel an INCREASED SEXUAL URGE after they stop smoking. Is it because of the increase in circulation? Is it because you have an extra hour a day with time on your hands? Or are you just using sex for a substitute? Who cares? It is a healthy substitute. You don't gain weight from it. More and more smokers are mentioning this side-effect of withdrawal.

Another side-effect not often mentioned that some smokers suffer from while going through nicotine withdrawal is constipation. There is controversy over whether this is emotional or physical. It doesn't really matter. Constipation can be corrected by drinking more water, exercising more, and taking extra bran in a salad, yogurt or juice. Your body's metabolism will soon be back in balance; this problem will disappear naturally.

10. **WHILE WITHDRAWING FROM CIGARETTES, YOUR MIND WILL PLAY TRICKS ON YOU.** You will be amazed at all the people who start talking in your head. You have only yourself—nicotine has a whole battalion. When nicotine says, "Oh, come on—you are an adult and capable of making the decision to have just one little cigarette," start talking to yourself.

Remind yourself that it only takes one little cigarette to become addicted all over again. So take your deep breaths, grab a substitute, or call someone who will talk you out of it. Or throw marsh-mallows at the wall!

11. **YOU WILL NOTICE THAT YOU TALK MORE WITHOUT YOUR CIGARETTES.** Friends, family, and co-workers will also notice that you talk more without your cigarettes. You bet! You've been putting the "cigarette plug" in your mouth rather than expressing your real feelings. You've been shutting yourself up for years.

When I first quit smoking and became an excessive talker, my family was about to beg me to go back to smoking. I kept apologizing for my outbursts, saying that "I'm just not myself." Well, who was I then? Just me—loud, clear and angry. After I had accepted these feelings as part of me, it took only about three weeks to learn to deal with the feelings in a more effective and positive way. By that time the flood of anger had slowed to a trickle, and I was really feeling good about the new verbal me. My marriage became better because I was more honest. My relation-ships with my children became much better because we communicated more honestly and openly. I no longer plugged up my true feelings. If this is a real problem, one you can't seem to deal with or that threatens important relationships, get professional help. It takes strength to ask for that help; be strong if you need it.

So many smokers with whom I worked are SUCCESSFUL because they looked upon with-drawal as something so terrible they kept reminding themselves of the fact when they wanted a cigarette: "But then I'd have to do this again, and I WON'T!" It kept them going—when you have the flu, you have no choice but to wait it out. Just when you're sure you're about to die, you recover. That's about what nicotine withdrawal amounts to. Just when you think you're about to give up, the nicotine leaves your system, and you start to remember what freedom feels like. Hang in there.

"She says we get to talk to ourselves, answer ourselves, and still not be declared mentally incompetent."

I like to quote a Chippewa Indian saying that goes like this: "Sometimes I go about pitying myself, and all the time I am being carried on great winds through the sky." This is a poetic way of saying that we sometimes wallow in self-pity when we are being cleansed, or healed. How can we get better if we haven't been worse? Think of your withdrawal period as a blessing. If you feel dizzy, just be glad that you are getting <u>more oxygen</u> to the brain to allow dizziness. It won't last forever, just until your body adjusts to its new level of health. If you feel sleepy the first week, just know it's because you're rid of the stimulant that kept your motor revving overtime. You'll balance out and get your energy back, but it will be a <u>natural</u> energy, not from the stimulation of nicotine. A glass of cold water by your side continually helps those with the problem. And withdrawal symptoms do eventually leave! Do you think any of us ex-smokers would have stayed off cigarettes if we were still in pain? I don't think anyone likes pain that much!

So, stick with it and come out a WINNER!

Directions for Relaxation Exercise

This is a relaxation exercise to help you quit smoking. It will help you be become more aware of how good relaxation can feel.

Always repeat your goals only in the <u>present</u> tense—"I am." Otherwise, your subconscious will accept it as a <u>future</u> desire, and it will never happen. Even if you are still a smoker, start practicing the exercise NOW . . . make it a new habit. You told yourself thousands of times that you were a smoker. You did this subconsciously every time you lit a cigarette . . . reverse the process!

All you need to do to practice this technique is to have someone read it to you while you are sitting comfortably with your eyes closed . . . or you can tape yourself on a tape recorder and play it as often as needed to reinforce your belief that you are an ex-smoker. This <u>is not</u> a deep, hypnotic state. It is a daydreaming state . . . you just add goal-setting to your daydreaming state. Please do not do this exercise while driving a car!

Sit comfortably with your eyes closed. Repeat the word "relax" to yourself, and imagine yourself in the most comfortable and safe place you have ever been. If you cannot recall a place from a pleasant experience, then put your imagination to work and design a place where you would like to be. <u>Let yourself have some fun</u>!!

FEELING COMFORTABLE WITHOUT CIGARETTES

I CAN IMAGINE MYSELF IN A <u>PLEASANT PLACE</u>. I <u>LIKE</u> BEING HERE. IT IS SAFE AND WARM HERE. I CAN COME HERE WHENEVER I FEEL STRESS OR THE NEED FOR A CIGARETTE. ALL I NEED TO DO TO GET HERE IS CLOSE MY EYES, AND TELL MYSELF THAT I AM IN MY PLEASANT PLACE. THERE IS NO SMOKING HERE. "I <u>AM</u> AN EX-SMOKER." I FEEL FREE WHEN I AM NOT SMOKING. I <u>LIKE</u> BEING IN CONTROL OF MY SMOKING HABIT. . . . NOW I AM GOING TO TAKE MY CIGARETTES, MY SMOKING HABIT, AND MY ASHTRAY AND STUFF THEM INTO A BIG YELLOW BALLOON. I QUICKLY TIE THE KNOT ON THE YELLOW BALLOON. IT SAILS OFF INTO THE SKY. IT IS GONE FOREVER . . . <u>IT IS TIME FOR MY SMOKING HABIT TO LEAVE MY LIFE</u>. THE YELLOW BALLOON HAS SAILED OFF INTO THE SKY, AND IT HAS MELTED INTO THE ATMOSPHERE. THE AIR IS PURE AND CLEAN HERE. THERE IS NO SMOKING HERE. MY LUNGS FEEL CLEAN AND PURE. I TAKE A DEEP BREATH, AND I CAN FEEL THE CLEAN AIR COMING INTO MY LUNGS. I <u>AM</u> AN EX-SMOKER. . . . I <u>AM</u> A THIN EX-SMOKER. . . . I <u>AM</u> FREE. . . . I AM IN CONTROL OF MY LIFE. . . . I AM <u>UNWILLING</u> TO BE A SMOKER. . . . ALL I NEED TO DO TO COME AWAY FROM MY PLEASANT PLACE IS TO OPEN MY EYES. . . . AND I FEEL RELAXED AND REFRESHED AND REVITALIZED.

Quitting Smoking and Retraining Yourself to Breathe

When we quit smoking, it isn't half as much fun to breathe. One <u>positive</u> thing we do when we inhale deeply on a cigarette is to practice the art of deep breathing; so when we quit smoking, it is very important that we relearn to deep breathe without the inhaling of a cigarette as the incentive. When we quit, we often find ourselves taking short and irregular breaths rather than deep and regular breaths. The body needs oxygen to exist, and proper breathing is what nourishes our body and keeps us in a more relaxed state of mind . . . and we certainly need some of that when we quit smoking.

<u>This is why cutting straws in half and "smoking" them serves not only as a safe oral and handling substitute, but as a retraining aid in the art of proper and efficient breathing</u>. If you "puff" on them once or twice a minute, you'll discipline yourself to deep breathe again. Please <u>do not</u> overdo this so you become lightheaded, dizzy, or you hyperventilate . . . just puff comfortably once or twice a minute as a reminder to deep breathe. It may take a month or two to retrain yourself in a new habit; you might even become addicted to straws!*

In my group sessions, I teach participants to "baby breathe." This is how we <u>all</u> started out breathing until we learned about breathing to the "tune" of a cigarette. Most of the smokers under 25 years of age still breathe correctly, but those of us who smoked for 15 years or longer need to relearn baby breathing. If you already breathe this way, you are lucky; if you don't it will be a little confusing . . . like patting yourself on the top of your head in an up and down motion, and patting your stomach at the <u>same</u> time in a "round-the-clock" motion.

*For obvious reasons, recovering cocaine users would not be advised to use straws as "substitutes" . . . "puffing" on an empty Aqua Filter would be more suitable.

Here's how you do it—as you breathe IN, you push your stomach OUT—this gets your stomach out of the way so that your lungs can take in a nice supply of air. Then as you exhale or breathe OUT, you pull your stomach IN which helps your lungs to expel air from the lungs more efficiently. Practice this exercise two or three times a day for a month or two until it becomes a normal breathing process.

When you have quit smoking, you will feel very <u>protective</u> of your lungs; you'll treasure fresh air knowing that your lungs now have a choice in the matter. When you have to be in situations where you are in smoke-filled rooms for extended periods of time, you can step outside and use the "baby breath" as a "cleansing breath." All you do is make sure that you inhale very <u>deeply</u> so as to adequately take in clean air and exhale with a forceful and exaggerated motion to adequately expel the smoke-contaminated air in your lungs.

Read the article, "Exercise and Smoking," in the Nutrition chapter—by doing exercise, you will also increase your <u>breathing</u> capacity, bring a fresh glow to your face, and FEEL GREAT again!

"When I catch myself wanting a cigarette, I realize it isn't really the <u>cigarette</u> I want. It is just a desire to bring back a certain comfortable feeling . . . or maybe a <u>lost</u> feeling of happiness or security."—Donna Gile, "A Successful ex-smoker"

"One of the rewards of quitting smoking was having renewed HOPE—hope that I could do anything—a good feeling about myself! One of the hardest parts of quitting smoking was being "hysterically up" or "hysterically down" during the first 3 months. My anger frightened me. I talked about these feelings to "safe" and supportive people. I <u>allowed</u> myself to feel angry and I began to accept it. I really thought I didn't have any anger—until I quit smoking. I TOOK A LOT OF WARM BATHS AND LISTENED TO RELAXATION TAPES TO NURTURE MYSELF."—Patty Merrill—1½ year recovery

It Does Get Better!

"At 21 days, you are 95% there.
At 3 months, you are 99% there.
At 1 year, you are 99.5% there.
The rest of your life you are 99.5% there.
The remaining .5% is what keeps us from relapsing.
The remaining .5% is the <u>fear</u> & <u>respect</u> for the drug Nicotine . . .
*   the insidious seduction of Nicotine!*
It is this self-awareness that will keep you enjoying the freedom &
*   self-respect of a nicotine-free life."*

V

Stress Management

When the initial stress of giving up smoking has subsided, you will want to learn new techniques for managing the stress of everyday living as an ex-smoker—WITHOUT LIGHTING UP A CIGARETTE. If we plan to be realistic about staying off cigarettes permanently, we need to be prepared to deal with future stress situations that have nothing to do with smoking. This chapter deals directly with the subject of stress. It is important that everyone learn to manage stress, not just ex-smokers. This is why I asked two educators to contribute their knowledge of stress management to this chapter.

Stress cannot be measured scientifically because no two people will react exactly the same to a given situation. MY PLEASURE MAY BE YOUR STRESS, AND YOUR PLEASURE MAY BE MY STRESS. Though we differ on how we handle stress, I'm sure there is one thing we all agree on—stress is out there. It shows up in the form of a racing heartbeat, nervous sweating, clammy hands, "butterflies" in the stomach, headaches, tension in the neck and shoulders, an uninvited rash, or a compulsive urge to overindulge in food, drink, drugs, sex, or cigarettes!

1. **STRESS IS ALSO AN INDIVIDUAL MATTER.** You cannot compare your stress with your neighbor's or your co-worker's stress; each individual reacts differently. When the last child leaves home, some parents consider it a stressful situation; others consider it a blessing. It is the RESPONSE to a situation that shows whether you are the MASTER or the VICTIM of your life!

One person may be fired from a job and become passive and quietly slip into seclusion and depression. The next person may become aggressive and proceed to tear up the surroundings. Some people seem to feel they have gained status if they have more stress than their neighbor or co-worker—to the point of almost bragging about it. Wouldn't it be more constructive to derive status from learning how to manage stress in a positive way rather than worrying about who has more? A personal observation I've made is that those who truly have devastating, stressful situations in their lives don't go about comparing and complaining; they are too busy doing something about it. So, don't worry about who has more stress. Put simply, we need to "mind our own stress."

2. **STRESS CAN BE SELF-INFLICTED.** After awhile we get into the habit of feeling comfortable with it. We feel guilty if we find ourselves too tranquil. We are so busy complaining about being victimized by impossible tasks or responsibilities (or whatever) that we lose sight of the fact that we had a CHOICE when we took them on. It is true that we are often powerless against government controls, various rules, regulations, and social mores; this makes it all the more important that we become "masters in control" of the choices left to US. Another reason for getting in control of your smoking habit: It will remain a continuing source of satisfaction. There will always be situations which leave us feeling restricted, frustrated, "tied down"; by learning how to respond constructively and positively to them, we eventually gain the art of stress management.

I AM NOT advocating throwing all responsibility to the wind; just the one(s) we have taken on to "look better" rather than "feel better"—those with no intrinsic value for our state of well-being. And the very act of being responsible can sometimes relieve stress. Nothing is more stressful and tiring than continual procrastination or the evasion of responsibility. And it makes us feel guilty. No, the secret lies in the BALANCE.

We all agree we should "pay our rent" on planet Earth, but we don't need to take on unnecessary stress by paying the rent of those around us as well. For instance, when our children are old enough to pay their own way, we allow them to maintain their pride by teaching them to hold up their own end—it's called TOUGH LOVE.

We need to do our tasks well, but we don't need to become obsessed with perfection to the point of damaging our personal relationships and our own health. For ten years of my life I carried an imaginary "perfect card" in my wallet. My house was spotless, my children were spotless, my yard was weedless, my meals were costless (but incredibly nutritious), my marriage appeared flawless, and what it all added up to was STRESS. I had headaches, aching joints, tension in neck and shoulders, skin rashes, unnecessary fears, depression, expectations that could never be satisfied, personal goals that would never be reached and I felt scattered! I ate compulsively and was FAT; I chain-smoked three packs of cigarettes a day, I showed a smiling face to the world, but I was crying inside—and I was only 30 years old! What would the next 30 years bring? More of the same, no doubt, unless I made some changes. I threw away my "perfect card." What a relief! Half of my stress was caused by the fear that I might lose it . . . or not live up to it! I didn't want on my tombstone: "SHE WAS ALWAYS TRYING TO BE PERFECT, BUT WE NEVER KNEW HER." I liberated myself from compulsive perfection, and at the same time liberated my family and friends from having to live up to my unrealistic expectations. Today I am very happy "doing my best," but as ME, not as someone I think I should be . . . and not at the expense of love, laughter, living, crying, feeling, learning, and hoping. I've come to believe that this is true liberation from STRESS!

Smoking and Stress Management

Smoking is an indirect and very temporary way of dealing with a problem. If you are in a situation in which you feel very tense, smoking might seem to be an effective way to deal with that nervousness or anxiety. But a more positive and healthy solution to your problem would be to confront whatever is making you tense. Grabbing a cigarette to comfort you can keep you from learning how to deal directly with the various "stresses" in your life.

The following stress management tips are designed not only to help you succeed in the process of quitting smoking, but also to help you deal with stress throughout your entire life. Learning to live without cigarettes involves learning to cope effectively with stress.

1. Examine the stress in your life. Are the causes related to your job? Parenting? Finances? Unfulfilled dreams? Interpersonal relationships?

   How are you presently responding to these stressful situations? Are you satisfied with your coping methods, or do you see a need to change and improve your strategies.

   Examine closely your attitudes and feelings about the stress in your life. Consider making a commitment to learn positive methods of dealing with stress.

2. The best way to gain control of your hassles and worries is to put them in tangible form. Prepare a list of everything that is worrying you or getting you down—a "worry list."

   You will probably discover some problems are very real and important, some are not so serious, and some will take care of themselves without any attention (believe it or not!!).

   Someone once said that 80% of the things we worry about never happen, and 15% are out of our control, so 5% is what we need to deal with. That's not quite so overwhelming.

   State your problems in writing, consider the possible solutions or actions needed to solve each problem; then decide in which order you want to tackle them. Be sure and write down the plan of action to handle each problem, then try it out.

3. Learn and practice simple relaxation exercises daily for 10–20 minutes.

4. "Overload" can result from expecting too much of yourself and allowing others to make excessive demands on your time and energy. To avoid or reduce this type of stress you first need to manage your time by prioritizing your tasks, planning how you will carry them out and eliminating the less important tasks. This might involve learning to say "no" to yourself and to people around you. This might surprise a few people initially, but most folks prefer an honest "no" to a begrudging "yes." Learn to delegate responsibility by avoiding the "but I'm the only one who can do it well" routine. You might lose your chance to become a full-fledged martyr, but you'll definitely learn that there are other capable people in the world. Initially the job might be performed less than perfect (in your eyes), but you will adjust if you just learn to accept help.

5. Do you confuse boredom with relaxation! A truly relaxed person has no need for a cigarette. Boredom can be stressful, and cigarettes appear to relieve that feeling by giving the person something to do, or distracting them from dealing with the real problem—the need for a more stimulating and interesting life. If this describes you, then take this opportunity to inject new elements into your life in the form of hobbies, activities, friends, challenges.

6. Physical activity can be an excellent tool to prevent or reduce stress. Beware of becoming so wrapped up in your performance and competition with others in the activity you choose, such that the "remedy" just becomes another cause of stress in your life. The purpose of exercise in stress management is to enhance your feeling of well-being and to create positive feelings towards yourself—resulting in a more tranquil and positive state of mind and body.

7. Many people find at times that they have so many problems and concerns that it is next to impossible to concentrate on the ordinary tasks of life without feeling constantly worried, anxious and/or preoccupied. If you find yourself in this position, try setting aside a portion of your day as a "worry break"—10, 15, or 20 minutes specifically for worrying. Sometimes just knowing there is a planned time for worrying will alleviate the stress and allow you to get your mind off your problems.

8. "Anxious reactivity" is when a person obsessively "relives" a stressful situation after it has happened, or "catastrophizes" an event before it happens. If you find yourself engaged in such unproductive thoughts, you might try the technique of "thought-stopping." As soon as you become aware of this anxious reliving or catastrophizing, shout the word "STOP" to yourself—out loud if you dare—then turn to less stressful thoughts or activities.

9. Depression, resulting from low self-esteem and a faltering self-image, can be very stressful. Many people continually underrate themselves and their abilities, often losing sight of their many good qualities and characteristics in the process. Others focus on the negative aspects of their lives, and become mired in self-pity and martyrdom. Some humility is necessary and good, but too much can be damaging to one's self-esteem, and can lead to depression. If you see this tendency in yourself, try verbalizing your good points, and take note of the positive aspects of your life. Accept compliments when they come your way—don't belittle yourself by minimizing your accomplishments or characteristics that others admire. Don't wait for the world to recognize you. Recognize yourself and discover all the things there are to like about yourself.

10. Stress management is a skill and must be practiced and improved regularly. Combinations of exercise, relaxation, assertiveness, enhanced self-awareness and increased self-esteem can help you feel healthier and cope better with the daily pressures of life. Smoking does not control or reduce the stress in your life; it PREVENTS you from actively coping with stress.

Courtesy of Merrie Ziady, Health Educator
Portland, Oregon

Smoking and Anger

Everyone gets angry. Some people have so controlled themselves not to show anger openly that typically such a controlled person suffers from migraine headaches, asthma, ulcers, skin problems, etc. Smokers often suppress anger by lighting up, effectively "plugging" any expression of anger temporarily. Eventually, however, the hostility builds up and aggressive and hurtful behavior results. Expressions of anger are healthy things, and can be done constructively. An important step in non-destructive expressions of anger is to accept responsibility for your own feelings. It is you who feels the anger and that doesn't make the other person "stupid," an "S.O.B." or the cause of your feelings.

A physical expression of strong feelings is a good means for venting hostility. Banging the table, stomping the floor, crying, hitting a pillow (all in private, of course) are all good devices for releasing strong feelings without aggression toward another person.

The healthiest way to deal with anger is to exercise spontaneous expression when you feel it to prevent the build-up of anger and to avoid the typical smoker's response: lighting up. Some verbal expressions that others have found useful include:

"I am very angry."
"I strongly disagree with you."
"I'm very distressed by the whole thing."
"I think that is unfair."
"It bothers me a lot."
"I am becoming very mad."

The important thing is to express your angry feelings without hurting someone (physically or mentally) in the process. Too often people express anger, frustration or disappointment with another by cowardly, indirect, and unnecessarily hurtful methods. Lashing out at someone—"damn you—if you weren't such an idiot . . ."—will probably only make the situation worse; whereas,

"You know, this whole situation really upsets me" could possibly lead to a combined effort to seek a solution. A worsened situation will only increase your "need" for cigarettes by allowing frustration and tension to rear their ugly heads.

Smoking is both a cowardly and indirect response to anger. It is cowardly because it allows you to avoid the issue or problem that is creating the anger and indirect because, for many smokers, it is intended to translate as, "See, I'm angry—you've made me so upset that I need a cigarette—it's all your fault." Unfortunately, many people will not even take notice of anger expressed so indirectly. This, in turn, can lead to increased build-up of hostility and feelings of low self-esteem.

Honest, spontaneous, "gut-level" assertive expression will help to prevent such inappropriate and destructive anger. Go ahead, get angry! But develop a positive, assertive style for expressing it. Even the advertisements don't claim that cigarettes effectively express anger!!

Smoking Craving Suppression Drill

1. When you feel a definite craving for a cigarette, allow your mind to focus on the craving.

2. Think of a negative image of the effects of smoking on your body (e.g., your skin is becoming wrinkled and aged as nicotine and carbon monoxide circulate your body, your breath is foul-smelling, and people are turning away from you in disgust).

3. Wait until you feel the full unpleasantness of the negative imagery. At this point your urge or craving for a cigarette should be reduced.

4. Now do a relaxation drill. You will notice further reduction in any residual urge to smoke.

5. Complete the pleasant stage of relaxation with a positive image as a reward for your success in suppressing your urge to smoke (e.g., you feel clean fresh air flowing through your lungs; you are enjoying the smell of freshly cut roses).

Courtesy of MERRIE ZIADY, Health Educator
Portland, Oregon

Anger Assessment/Learning to Process Anger

IT IS O.K. TO <u>FEEL</u> ANGRY—WHAT I <u>DO</u> WITH MY ANGER MAY NOT BE O.K. Cigarettes may act as an "emotional plug". When we quit smoking, we may find suppressed anger is surfacing. This is the time to <u>accept</u> our anger and begin to discover what feelings lie <u>beneath</u> the anger. When we begin to understand our anger, we can learn to take POSITIVE <u>ACTION</u> rather than to give NEGATIVE <u>REACTIONS</u>.

When we pretend we aren't angry, we may become very sarcastic, critical, depressed or judgemental. We may pout ("silent violence"), or withhold affection or attention from the object of our anger.

This assessment is designed to help you explore what anger <u>means</u> to you, how you <u>act out</u> your anger and how you <u>REact</u> in angry situations. If dealing with your anger seems too overwhelming, seek a support group or professional guidance to support you as you explore your anger . . . this is just one more step to FREEDOM!

1. An angry person is someone who _____ .

2. In my family of origin, anger was expressed by _____ .

3. Was <u>my</u> right to anger denied or validated? _____ .

4. I act out my anger by: POUTING ("Silent Violence"), YELLING, TEASING, TEARS. Or by being SARCASTIC, CRITICAL OR JUDGEMENTAL; by SMOKING, OVER-EATING/DRINKING, DRUGS, DISTANCING, ABRUPTNESS. Or with DEPRESSION or DENIAL OF ANGER _____ .

5. Does acting out my anger in the above manner work for me? _____ .

   What are the "payoffs" for my current behavior? _____ .

6. How do others react to my anger? _____ .

   How do I justify my anger? _____ .

7. How long do I usually remain angry? _____ . Why? _____ .

8. When others are angry at me, I feel _____ .

9. The types of people who make me very angry are _____ .

   The events/assaults that make me very angry are _____ .

10. I am able to accept my angry self: YES _____ NO _____

Sources

Lerner, Harriet G. *The Dance of Anger.* New York: Harper & Row. 1986.

Tavris, Carol. *Anger—The Misunderstood Emotion.* New York: Simon & Schuster. 1983.

ASK YOURSELF THESE QUESTIONS TO IDENTIFY THE FEELINGS <u>BENEATH</u> THE ANGER:

- <u>WHAT AM I AFRAID OF LOSING</u>? Anger often "masks" the fear that we are losing something/someone important to us. . . . Control . . . Cigarettes . . . Dignity . . . Image . . . Relationship . . . Power . . . Money . . . Respect, etc. For example, if we are angry when our child breaks a curfew, are we really afraid of losing <u>parental control</u>—or losing our <u>child</u>? By <u>sharing</u> our fears, communication lines will open—anger "melts".

- <u>HOW CAN I GET DOWN TO THE ACTUAL PAIN OR HURT</u>? If I can allow myself to feel the pain, I begin to escape chronic anger. It is <u>healthy</u> to hurt—then begin the process of healing. It is <u>unhealthy</u> to deny the pain—the pain becomes anger, resentment, depression, revenge and assorted physical ailments. What sadness am I afraid of? What pain am I allowing to "fester"?

- <u>WHO OR WHAT AM I TRYING TO CONTROL/CHANGE</u>? Is this person/event <u>worth</u> my daily stress energy? Can I really <u>change</u> this person/event? Can I make a difference by remaining angry? How? If this person/event gets <u>worse</u>, do I get <u>angrier</u>?

- <u>HAS MY INTEGRITY/DIGNITY BEEN ASSAULTED</u>? How? By whom? For example if someone ridicules your moral values or beliefs, <u>you have a right to feel angry</u>. <u>Then allow yourself to feel the pain</u>. When your values or beliefs are assaulted, your "real self" has been assaulted—of course it hurts! Allow the hurt, consider the source, take positive action if needed, seek support or counsel, and allow yourself adequate healing time.

- <u>WHAT IS MY ANGER</u>? When I learned to process my anger, I realized that I always got angry when I <u>cared too much</u> (My CARING SELF) or when I <u>felt judgemental</u> (My JUDGEMENTAL SELF). I learned to "embrace" and accept these parts of myself so that I can now foresee when they will become "overactive" and turn into anger. I HAVE LEARNED TO <u>CARE</u> WHERE I CAN MAKE A DIFFERENCE! If I can't make a difference, I have learned to let my anger go. I HAVE LEARNED TO <u>JUDGE</u> ONLY IF I AM WILLING TO BE JUDGED. These two tasks will only take a lifetime. WHAT IS YOUR ANGRY SELF? Do I expect so much perfection from myself/others that my anger is my PERFECTIONISTIC SELF? My CONTROLLING SELF? My FRIGHTENED SELF? My HURTING SELF? My VULNERABLE SELF? My MARTYR SELF? My INSECURE SELF? My UNREALISTIC SELF? Be self-responsible!! Take responsibility for control issues hurt, pain, fear and insecurities . . . doing this brings us down to our real feelings. When we are responsible for our <u>real feelings</u>, genuine communication and personal growth take place.

Give yourself time to learn how to process your anger. <u>Learn</u> from the mistakes you make. Ask those who are affected by your anger to be gentle with you as you relearn the process of knowing yourself. <u>Be gentle with yourself—you are worth it!</u>—Linda R. Bryson

"There are certain times I just can't remember my coping skills."

Everyday Stress Situations and Some Coping Alternatives

A. *SOMEONE AHEAD OF YOU DOESN'T MOVE FORWARD THE <u>SPLIT SECOND</u> THAT THE LIGHT TURNS GREEN AT A STOP LIGHT. . . .*

<u>AND</u>: You have a <u>choice</u> in how you react: You can honk at them, turn beet-red in the face, and fantasize about them dropping dead at the next stoplight. You may waste your day's energy quota on them, and raise your own blood pressure significantly.

<u>OR</u>: You can give them the benefit of the doubt as to why they move slowly—perhaps they just suffered a tragedy, they are sick, or they are just having a lousy day. Maybe being honked at "turns them on," and <u>you</u> just made someone a little happier.

<u>YET</u>: You might find it advisable to stop off at a bookstore and buy a copy of "Type A Behavior and Your Heart"; perhaps you can learn why <u>your</u> stress tolerance is so low. Then notice that the world is <u>still revolving</u>; maybe <u>one</u> split second of your life being held up at a stop light will not be very significant to you fifty years from now.

B. *SOMEONE BEHIND YOU HONKS AT YOU BECAUSE YOU AREN'T MOVING FORWARD AT RACING SPEED WHEN THE LIGHT TURNS GREEN.*

AND: You have a choice in how you react: You can turn around and make an ugly face, use finger symbols, or honk back. You may waste your day's energy quota on that driver, and raise your own blood pressure significantly.

OR: You can smile and wave at them, which not only lowers your blood pressure, but helps to relieve their stress because they are now busy trying to figure out where they have known you. Or you can feel sorry for them because they are "Type A" behavior people; you can be grateful that you don't have to live in their nervous body.

YET: You could cut down on your day-dreaming at stop lights.

C. *SOMEONE CUTS IN FRONT OF YOU ON THE HIGHWAY.*

AND: You have a choice in how you react: You can hate them at first sight. You can honk at them 50 times. You can turn beet-red. You can waste your day's energy quota on them, and raise your own blood pressure significantly.

OR: You might realize that if you are still able to feel mad, you are also still alive; try being GRATEFUL. You can take a couple of deep breaths, and repeat the word "RELAX" to yourself. You can pat yourself on the back for your wonderful defensive driving. Because you are still alive, you can take it as a sign that you were intended for great things on this earth.

YET: You might take out your wallet or purse and see if you have your "PERFECT CARD" with you . . . have you been perfect on the highway? Remember how STUPID you felt when you were distracted or day-dreaming and did the same thing? Remembr how you wished you could evaporate? Remember how you wished you could write a 1,000-word theme of valid excuses for being so HUMAN and hand it to the person you offended? Chances are that is about how they are feeling

D. *YOU ARE TIRED OF PICKING UP AFTER FAMILY MEMBERS!*

AND: You have a choice in how you react: You can nag at them continually to no avail. You can play the role of the MARTYR and "do it yourself." You can let the mess pile up until it disgusts even them—WHICH IT WON'T!

OR: You can try what my sister (who has nine children) did: She found that the things left laying around were always the family's "favorite things," so she gathers them into boxes, stores them elsewhere, and the children will have a wonderful holiday when they receive the boxes of "favorite things" at Christmas time. How can she go wrong with the choices when they are the children's "favorite things"? When the children saw that she intended to follow this plan, the house became mysteriously clutterfree. Or you can let the children know that although you understand they don't like "picking up," WHATEVER GAVE THEM THE IDEA THAT YOU DO?!? Or you can explain that you need their help. Children "tune out" NAGGING, but "tune in" being NEEDED.

YET: This is a problem that will never be solved <u>completely</u> because families aren't perfect . . . SO WHY DO <u>MOTHERS</u> HAVE TO BE? Are we being sensibly organized, or are we being COMPULSIVE? Nobody ever died from "dirty socks" on the floor—they only die from the <u>stress</u> it <u>creates</u>! Are we trying to impress our neighbors instead of our family? Do we have enough outside interests and hobbies that we can <u>let up on ourselves</u>? Can we realize that SUPERMOMS/DADS "wear out" very quickly?

E. SOME PEOPLE ARE ALWAYS LATE AND CAUSE ME GREAT STRESS.

AND: You have a <u>choice</u> in how you react: You can "get crazy" while you wait for them. You can tell them to "hurry up" 20–30 times which frustrates you so much when it <u>doesn't</u> work that you have a terrible time when you get to where you're going.

OR: You can accept that "slow people" go even <u>more</u> slowly when pushed, and if they do make it on time, they'll be minus a shoe or sock. Since it's obvious after 10 years of this that you're going to have to play the waiting game with them, why not have a good time of it—call the family in for a sing-a-long, or pound out a happy song on the piano to relieve <u>your</u> tension in a positive way, or read another chapter in that book you've been trying to finish, or do a relaxation exercise since you definitely have some time to spare! You could try leaving without the late person(s) but it would just make everyone, including you, feel uncomfortable in the long run.

YET: <u>Always</u> being late shows disrespect for some else's time, so you might have them read "The Angry Book" which calls chronic lateness "subtle sabotage"; you might ask them to be open with you and tell you what is <u>really</u> making them ANGRY.

F: MY CHILDREN ARE NOT LIVING UP TO <u>MY</u> GREAT EXPECTATIONS.

AND: You have a <u>choice</u> in how you react: You can disown them. You can run away from home. You can become paranoid and think that <u>everyone</u> is talking about your children. You can constantly belittle them until they <u>live up</u> to your belittling. You can go into hiding.

OR: You can quit living their lives for them. You can start living your <u>own</u> life. You can give them back the freedom to make mistakes while becoming what <u>they</u> want to be. If they are as smart and gifted as <u>you</u> believe they are, they are probably smart enough to know what they want to do with their lives. IF THEY ARE NOT LIVING UP TO YOUR EXPECTATIONS, AT LEAST BE GRATEFUL THEY ARE <u>LIVING</u>! It has been said "IT IS <u>IMPOSSIBLE</u> TO BE RESENTFUL AT THE SAME TIME YOU ARE BEING GRATEFUL." Look for their good qualities and support their growth; quit magnifying their bad qualities to the point that they <u>might</u> become reality! Ask yourself why you find it necessary to <u>pick</u> your childrens' careers and futures when <u>they</u> are the ones who must live, work, and cope with them. Be grateful if your child wants to be a mechanic or a carpenter as long as he/she is <u>happy</u> with that choice. I really believe bad workmanship and poor quality in products and crafts would be a thing of the past if <u>everyone</u> was doing what they wanted to to do and what they do BEST. I like the story about a very <u>peaceful</u> <u>carpenter</u>, born about 2000 years ago. I'm so glad his parents didn't force him into a career he hated. I'm sure that the messages he gave to the world would <u>not</u> have been <u>positive</u> messages if he had not been doing what he WANTED to be doing.

You can question your own life. Why is it so incomplete that you tend to live it through another human being? No one can be expected to live up to your unfulfilled dreams when they have their own set of dreams to be fulfilled. We can learn to understand that we put unfair burdens upon those with whom we live and work if we put our expectations on them; we are guaranteed to be disappointed. Let's learn what their dreams are. Let's help them to develop their natural talents and abilities in a purely supportive way. Sure . . . they'll fall on their faces a few times getting there, but what's important is that we are available with love and support to help them get back on their feet and back into the race.

YET: This is much easier said than done, and it takes practice and patience with ourselves as we learn this new habit. If you find this difficult to do alone, get professional help. You'll find your children will not "discard you" when you become old and need their support . . . and you will have their RESPECT and LOVE.

Change can be fun if we take time for an "attitude readjustment." We remain "victims" of negative habits only because we CHOOSE to.

Recommended Readings

Benson, Herbert, M.D. *Beyond the Relaxation Response*. New York: Berkley Publishing Co. 1985.
Braiker, Harriet B., Ph.D. *The Type E* Woman*. New York: Dodd, Mead & Co. 1986.

Basic Stress Theory

STRESSORS	PLUS	PERCEPTIONS OR BELIEF SYSTEMS	EQUAL	STRESS
Stressors		*Perceptions or Belief Systems*		*Stress*
Stressors are the ACTIVATING EVENTS or the "TIGERS" that we encounter in our daily lives. Every time we are faced with a stressor, our body prepares us for "fighting the tigers." This process is known as the "fight or flight" response. Stressors may be negative or positive. Although falling in love can be a positive stressor, it may cause our heart to beat faster and there seems to be a constant rush of adrenalin. An end to a loving relationship usually is a negative stressor. Examples of stressors are listed below: Environmental Stressors: Quitting smoking • Divorce • Separation • Work pressure • School pressure • Crowds •		Our perceptions are the ways in which we sense or interpret an event; also the way in which we sense or interpret stressors to be negative or positive. For example, if we interpret or sense that water is a positive element, we will perceive taking swimming lessons as a positive stressor. By the same token, if we interpret or sense that water is a "dangerous" element because we almost drowned as a child, we might be inclined to perceive swimming lessons as a negative stressor. An obese person may consider swimming lessons a negative stressor because he/she has a belief system that states: "I am fat and therefore I don't want anyone to see me in a bathing suit." In other words, taking swimming lessons may be a positive stressor for one person and a negative stressor for another person. Our Belief Systems are internal processes that are developed over long periods of time. They are derived from the "life messages" that we choose to believe. Belief systems can cause us to think, feel, and act in a certain pattern. There are positive belief systems that we want to cherish and there are negative belief systems that cause us undue stress because they are unrealistic and destructive. I have listed some with questions to ask yourself:		Stress is our REACTION. When we are confronted with a stressor, we may react with fear, anger, hostility, joy, pain, sadness, depressions, drug or alcohol abuse, overeating, or disappointment, etc. WE DO HAVE CHOICES IN HOW WE REACT. If a loved one dies, of course the reaction will be loss, grief, etc. But, there is a choice in whether we go on and rebuild our own lives or we remain locked in "Why me?," anger and resentment.

Basic Stress Theory

STRESSORS	PLUS	PERCEPTIONS OR BELIEF SYSTEMS	EQUAL	STRESS
Stressors		*Perceptions or Belief Systems*		*Stress*
Weather • Noise • Traffic • Deadlines • Exams • Confrontations • Transitions • Job security • Job loss • Children • Parents • Mates • Financial insecurities • Death of mate or loved one. Psychological Stressors: Thought processes and feelings (hate, fear, anxiety, anger, revenge, depression, grudges, self-pity, loneliness, regrets, inadequacy) • Relationships (interpersonal or communication processes). Physiological Stressors: Illness • Aging • Adolescence • Disease • Injuries • Lack of food / sleep/exercise • Chronic pain.		"I must be perfect." [or Who might reject you?] • "I should please everyone." [Who made that rule?] • "My mate/children/friends should be perfect." [What planet do you come from?] • "I must be perfectly thin." [Will you then be perfectly loved?] • "The world should be perfectly peaceful." [Am I?] • "I am inadequate, ugly and unloved." [Who told you that lie?] • "My house should always be clean." [or Who might reject you?] • "My children should become what I want them to be." [Did I postpone my own dreams and goals so I must live through them?] "I must be a perfect provider." [Who am I failing if I am not?]		Stress is how we act after we have given MEANING to the event or how we PERCEIVE the event. If someone cuts us off on the freeway, we can either interpret the driver's cutting in front of us as a personal attack, certain that they were out stalking "special me" on the freeway, just to ruin my day or we may decide not to waste our stress energy on an event we can not change! The stress may be short- or long-term. It is the long-term stress that is so disabling to body, mind and soul.

How to Keep a Stress Log

    Keep a record of stressful events that happen in your daily life. Here is a system you can use after you read about <u>STRESSORS</u>, BELIEF SYSTEMS/PERCEPTIONS, and STRESS/ REACTIONS.

1. Identify the STRESSOR. The stressor may be <u>Environmental</u> (weather, noise, work-related, etc.); <u>Physiological</u> (illness, pain, injuries, etc.); <u>Thought Processes</u> (feelings such as anger, fear, guilt, etc.).

2. Then write down the resulting STRESS/REACTION that you felt. How did you interpret the event? Was there an incident from the past that always causes you to react the same way? Why? How did it make you feel?

3. Now note how you PHYSICALLY felt the stress such as: Headache • Stomachache • Tension in the jaw • Tension in the neck and shoulder area • Backache • Skin rash • Constipation • Diarrhea • Aching joints or muscles • Gastro-intestinal disturbances • Shortness of breath • Tightness in throat. . . .

4. Next list what possible BELIEF SYSTEMS might have been responsible or influential in determining how you reacted to the event:

   "Life <u>should be</u> fair."   "I <u>must</u> be perfect at all times."
   "My mate <u>should</u> meet all my needs."   "Quitting smoking <u>ought</u> to be easy."
   "I <u>should</u> be perfectly thin."   "Everyone <u>should</u> understand me."
   "Everyone <u>should</u> appreciate me."   "The world <u>should</u> be perfect."
   "Nice people <u>must not</u> feel angry."   "I <u>must</u> please everyone . . . always."
   "My house <u>must</u> be spotless."   "I <u>should</u> always be cheerful and out-
                                            going."

   "I <u>must</u> do <u>all</u> the work because I'm the <u>only</u> one who does it right!"
   [Notice the "shoulds," "oughts," and "musts" that rule us!]

5. Next list what possible PERCEPTIONS might have been responsible or influential in determining <u>how</u> you reacted to the event.

   "I perceive that a rejection (stressor) means that I am not worthwhile."
       (<u>Who</u> are you still reacting to from the past?)
   "I perceive that making a mistake means that I am a failure."
       (Who told you that one? Did they also tell you mistakes are how we <u>learn</u>?)
   "I perceive that any change will be too frightening to handle."
       (It's OK to be afraid—what you <u>do</u> with your fear might not be OK for you.)

6. What more positive BELIEF SYSTEMS/PERCEPTIONS might I adopt to start reacting differently?

"Life isn't fair, but I will be OK."

"There are some people I will <u>never</u> please—and I won't die from that!"

"I am still a worthwhile person—even when I get rejected."

"I can't meet <u>all</u> my mate's needs, so how can my mate meet <u>all</u> of mine?"

   (<u>Who</u> made that dumb rule that a mate must meet <u>all</u> our needs?)

"If I can please people 50% of the time, I'm doing great!"

"Quitting smoking isn't easy, but I am strong and capable of reaching my goal."

"The world <u>is</u> perfect—there are just lots of people giving it a bad name."

7. State your new BELIEF SYSTEM/PERCEPTION over and over again until it becomes a new habit. You will begin to react more automatically in the new manner, like being "on pilot" when you drive a car.

8. Have UNDERSTANDING that changing habits/beliefs takes from 30 days to a lifetime before it is automatic behavior. How long did it take you to become a stressful person? An addicted person? How long are you willing to give yourself to create a new lifestyle? If you want to be "fixed" overnight, it <u>will</u> take a lifetime because this is an unrealistic BELIEF. Allow yourself the time it <u>realistically</u> takes and it will happen—YOU ARE WORTH THE TIME!

Stressor or event: _____

_____

_____

_____

Resulting stress or reaction: _____

_____

_____

_____

Physical reaction: _____

_____

_____

_____

Belief system/perception that keeps me reacting in a negative manner to a stressful situation:

_____

_____

_____

What is more realistic/positive belief system or perception that I might adopt to start reacting differently: _____

_____

_____

_____

What keeps me from changing my old patterns? What am I afraid of losing? What is the worst that could happen if I change? _____

_____

_____

_____

What support system/person can I depend upon to support me while I make the positive changes?

_____

_____

What is the first step I will take to change my reaction? _____

_____

How long do I give myself to make the positive changes? (Be realistic and gentle with yourself.)

_____

_____

_____

_____

Linda R. Bryson
© 1985

Behavior and Feelings that Reduce the Stress Response

1. **Relaxation. Prayer. Centering. Meditation. Focusing.** (15–30 minutes daily).
2. **Aerobic exercise** such as walking, jogging, bicycling, swimming, cross-country skiing, trampoline, aerobic dance, rowing. (15–45 minutes at least 3 times weekly at target heart rate). Be sure to check with your physician first.
3. **Assertion.** (Knowing your rights and expressing them in an assertive manner—please do not confuse with aggression.)
4. **Structure.** (Creating parts of your life so they fall into regular and familiar patterns to provide stability.)
5. **Consistency.** (Acting out the pattern in harmonious and regular manner to provide safety and belonging.)
6. **Warmth.** (Dilates blood vessels—more blood flow to extremities.)
7. **Eating.** (Done with moderation and in relaxed atmosphere.)
8. **Human touch and hugging.** (Need I explain?)
9. **Holding or caring for an animal or pet.** (They love us just as we are!)
10. **Preparation.** (Knowing you are prepared; helps to relieve anxiety.)
11. **Laughter.** (Similar positive after-effect, such as moderate exercise.)
12. **Crying.** (May help restore proper body chemistry after stressful or painful situation.)
13. **Escaping** into a good book, movie or television show. (Takes mind off self; is a mini-vacation of the mind.)
14. **Self-acceptance.** (Reduces stress response occurring from unrealistic self-expectation.)
15. **Self-responsibility.** (Owning your faults as well as your perfections—finding more people to blame can be stressful, especially when you finally run out of people.)
16. Allowing yourself to **give to others.** (Feels especially good when you don't expect anything in return or "keep count.")
17. Allowing yourself to **receive from others.** (Eliminates the stress from having to reject someone's caring.)
18. **Surrender.** (Releasing the need to control other people as that is their business in the first place.)
19. **Having a sense of purpose** or meaning in your life. (Knowing that pain and joy can be opportunities to learn and grow . . . or excuses to stop learning and growing.)
20. **Having an "attitude of gratitude."** There is nothing wrong with the world; it has always been beautiful . . . there are just too many people in it acting ugly!
21. **Accomplishing a physical task.** When so much of our lives seem scattered and "in the middle," cleaning a closet, scrubbing a floor, weeding a flower bed, completing something creative or mowing a lawn will give us the experience of finishing something, a fulfilling sense of accomplishment.

Linda R. Bryson
© 1984

Sometimes we procrastinate because we are afraid we might not do something perfectly—like quitting smoking. Or we quit smoking and we are afraid to start new projects or goals—which we need to fill in the void left by the smoking habit. We are afraid to "follow our dreams." This assessment was designed to take you through the process of procrastination so that you can better understand it—then take action to modify it so that you are no longer paralyzed by it!

The Three Ps of Procrastination

1. PERFECTIONISM ("I can't start because it might not be perfect.")
2. PROCRASTINATION ("I'll sit here and think it to perfection.")
3. PARALYSIS ("Now I'm perfectly stuck.")

- *ASK YOURSELF THESE QUESTIONS TO UNDERSTAND YOUR PROCRASTINATION:*

A. Doing something perfectly means that I am _____ .

B. Making a mistake means that I am _____ .

C. What might happen if I make a mistake?

D. Making a mistake is an assault to my _____ .

E. Who might reject me if I make a mistake? (List persons)
F. Who in the past rejected me when I made a mistake? (List persons)
G. Do these people from the past still have power over me? How?

H. When I see others making mistakes, I think they are _____ .

I. When I procrastinate, I feel _____ .

J. What is the "payoff" or purpose of not starting a project?
K. Is the "payoff" of procrastination self-destructive/productive?
L. Whom do I control or "make crazy" by not starting a project?

M. When I am into paralysis (perfectly stuck), I feel _____ .

N. What planet do people come from who make no mistakes?

Linda R. Bryson
© 1984

- *PLAN OF ACTION FOR PROCRASTINATORS:*

A. SET REALISTIC GOALS. Procrastinators often expect so much out of themselves they set goals that are impossible to achieve. (Depression can result from unrealistic expectations and goals.)

B. INCREASE YOUR TIME FOR COMPLETION. If you ordinarily give yourself 3 weeks for a certain project (which might be realistic for non-procrastinators or non-perfectionists), then give yourself 6 weeks to finish. DECREASE THE DURESS (pressure) TO INCREASE YOUR SUCCESS!

C. DO NOT COMPARE YOURSELF WITH NON-PERFECTIONISTS OR OTHERS. Your learning style, style, and timing style are unique to you. You may improve or modify your style, but trying to be someone else is guaranteed to lead to fear, depression and lowered self-worth.

D. START! It is O.K. to be afraid! How we act out our fear may not be O.K. for us. Making a mistake by starting only means that we were willing to make a change from our procrastination pattern. If you make a mistake, admit it, and ask yourself what you learned from the mistake. YOU ARE STILL A WORTHWHILE PERSON.

E. START GIVING YOURSELF NEW AFFIRMATIONS AND "SELF-TALK":
   1. "I am a worthwhile person—even when I make mistakes."
   2. "My mistakes are my learning—part of my personal history."
   3. "I am worthwhile—even if others reject me for my mistakes."
   4. "I can start my project now and risk making a mistake, or I can procrastinate and risk losing my self-worth and self-esteem."
   5. "I'll do my personal best—leaving perfection for those who have already ascended."
   6. "I live on Planet Earth—where mistakes are created and buried."

How to Write and Use an Affirmation for Change

What is an affirmation? An affirmation means to "say YES." When we form self-destructive or negative patterns in our lives, perhaps we are actually saying "NO" to our positive and healthy self. An affirmation is just one of many tools which help us to say "YES" to ourselves again.

Once we choose to change or modify our behavior, we need to realize that it took us many years to develop and maintain our <u>current</u> behavior. In order to make a change that is permanent and compatible to our personal belief system, we need to allow ourselves a reasonable period to time (from 30 days to 2 years) before we are on "automatic." We are on "automatic" when we drive a car—we don't even have to <u>think</u> about it. We need to also make the change in a positive manner (rather than one that is forced or threatening) so we feel the change is our own personal choice.

<u>Consciously</u> and logically, we can say that we want to change our lifestyle or behavior, but it is at the <u>sub-conscious</u> level that patterned behavior is stored—and acted upon. Affirmations are just positive messages that we give to ourselves until we begin to BELIEVE them—when we begin to believe them, we begin to act them out. After acting them out long enough, they become new habits or part of our current belief system.

1. *<u>USE ONLY THE PRESENT TENSE</u>*. The sub-conscious takes commands and messages <u>literally</u>. If you incorrectly word the affirmation, "I will be an ex-smoker tomorrow," the command is future-oriented and will never be realized. State the affirmation as "I <u>am</u> a healthy ex-smoker," or "I <u>am</u> a thin ex-smoker," or "I <u>am</u> slim and weigh 120 pounds," or "I <u>am</u> feeling calm and relaxed."

2. *<u>STATE THE AFFIRMATION IN A POSITIVE MANNER—DO NOT USE NEGA-TIVES</u>*. If you incorrectly state the affirmation, "I can't eat candy or pie," you are using the negative "can't" which is about as effective as telling someone, "Don't you <u>dare</u> think about pink elephants." State the affirmation as "I visualize myself eating only healthy foods that give nourishment to my body," or "I choose to eat nourishing foods," or "Every day I enjoy my relaxation."

3. *<u>TO RELEASE NEGATIVE THOUGHT PATTERNS</u>*. A sentence or affirmation that is helpful in getting rid of self-destructive thought processes is, "I am willing to release my need for _____ ." Fill in the blank with negative words such cigarettes, overeating, anger, revenge, hate, fear, etc.

4. *<u>BE SPECIFIC AND ON TARGET</u>*. If you wish to get along better with your family and not see only their <u>faults</u>, state the affirmation, "I see myself enjoying my family and recognizing their <u>positive</u> traits." Negative traits are <u>easy</u> to perceive. It takes love, understanding and retraining to see primarily the positive traits. If you wish to start aerobic exercise on a regular basis, state the affirmation, "I visualize myself exercising 25 minutes daily and enjoying the benefits that I receive in self-esteem and fitness."

5. *<u>PRACTICE WITH REGULARITY</u>*. State your affirmations at least twice daily. After 30 days, they will be a habit and "automatic." Do them while waiting in lines . . . while driving the car . . . before personal and business interactions . . . before falling asleep at night. Keep them posted around the house (and office) where you will be sure to see them (for instance, on the mirror of your medicine cabinet).

Change

How much energy
   we are willing to exert
   when fighting the aging process
   of our bodies . . .

Yet

   How little energy
we are willing to exert
when fighting the aging process
of our minds.

                       LRB

scripsit gm castor 1983

VI
Making Changes

"Change is the beginning of growth."—L. B.

WISDOM tells us that "change is the only constant." Except birth and death, it does seem to be the only guarantee that life hands out, so let's go with that eternal guarantee called change.

Of course, the process of giving up cigarettes will be the biggest change you will make. IT WILL BE THE FIRST CHANGE YOU MAKE. Then you will make many more changes if you wish to stay off cigarettes. An example of this will be if you are one of the people who really believes that your car won't start until you light your cigarette, you will have to make a change. You will have to start telling yourself that lighting up a cigarette has nothing to do with starting your car. You'll then fill your ashtray with mints, gum, or straws as the second change. By stopping smoking, reprogramming your thought processes, and making the ashtray symbolic of something besides the SMOKING habit, you will have incurred three changes. This can only lead to success if you reinforce it.

Successful people know the value of change, how to use it, how to capitalize on it, how not to fear it. Because of the way successful people change, their goals and ideas and actions always point to the future. For change guarantees that the future will come upon us sooner than we expected. This does not mean that we can ever take today or tomorrow for granted. It just means that if today is completed and tomorrow comes, there will be change. Successful people do not deal in the past. There is nothing they can do about it. Why waste the energy?

If you choose to quit smoking, you will be looking to a future goal as an ex-smoker. You will make changes in order to become an ex-smoker. If you are not willing to make changes in your life to become an ex-smoker, you will remain a smoker.

Have you ever noticed that some people retire and start making changes than enable them to have the time of their lives? They travel and finish the dreams that they never before had time to finish. They make changes. Even if there is fear, they overcome the fear, and reach out and achieve success in their retirement. They learn to play again. Then there are the people who fear change so much that when they retire, they just retire to their chairs. Someone else gave them the idea that their lives were through, and they believed it. They become depressed, ill, and full of self-pity. They take up the "woe is to me" syndrome and wonder why people avoid them. They become even more lonely. Death becomes the only change to which they look forward. And their wishes are granted. Successful retirees know that "if you rest it, it rusts." They make changes that will enable them to keep active, not only physically but mentally. They do not believe in self-induced senility.

Have you also noticed how some people, when losing a spouse either to death or divorce, will mourn for awhile, regain their sense of direction, pick themselves up, and get back in the race?

"The race" is life. And winning the race is knowing that one must go on. Learn the beauty of "being alone, but not lonely"—trusting enough to love again—being of service—and thinking about the present and future, not the past. Those who already live their lives that way seem to take losses and changes more easily. They've been running the race as winners for a long time—they can accept a loss or change in pace and survive! Those who have been in the race but were running in a rut will not take a loss or change of pace so easily. When they experience a loss or change, they stop looking forward. They start running backward. But the past gives no comfort. Only memories. Memories can be warm and beautiful, but we starve emotionally if we try to live on them as a steady diet. And when we can't accept change, we become depressed. We become criers of doom. And if we search for doom long enough, doom wll begin to follow. Doom seems to favor those who cherish it.

The moral to this tale is that when you give up cigarettes, it will be a loss and a big change in your life. You can allow yourself to mourn that loss, but you'll eventually have to accept the fact that the loss is your gain—your gain in health, life and self-mastery. You'll go on, and you'll have made such a big change that you probably will be motivated to make some more positive changes in your life. It seems to be the beginning of a very exciting way of life. Keep reminding yourself that this experience is a beginning as well as an ending.

When I quit smoking, I had such a burst of self-pride that it propelled me to fight my lifelong battle with weight. After tackling the battle with weight, I knew I could have the courage to go back to college as a 35-year-old freshman. Was it easy? No—but because I'd made other changes that were difficult and had succeeded, I knew I could do it. I had to do a lot of talking to myself and it was all positive in nature. I had to keep telling myself, "You can do it," "You will do it!"—I'm still doing it, and I'm no longer afraid. Also going back to school gave me the confidence to make other big and positive changes in my life. It all started because I made the change to stop smoking. That is called a chain of events. It all starts with one step.

The main advantage to making changes a way of life is that when one is thrown your way unexpectedly, you'll feel more familiar with ways of surviving and accepting the temporary turmoil and pain that it may bring.

While working with people in my stop-smoking programs, I noticed that the proportion of fear of change was consistent with how long it had been since they had made major changes. Those with the least fear were young people and they are easier to help for this reason. They are already in constant change because of their energy and age. I remember how many changes I experienced from age 15 to age 25. I wanted to "get older" so I could get in to a comfortable rut for "a change." I got in my rut, and stopped changing. Then I started fearing change and hiding from it. But it wouldn't go away. When I decided to stop smoking, I stopped fearing change. Now I look forward to change. Not that I still don't tremble and hesitate for awhile before taking that first step—that is normal. The point is, I no longer fear the aging process, because I no longer fear change. Isn't that all there really is to aging?

So, of course, it is usually easier for younger people to quit smoking than older people. The younger ones may resent the changes they have to make, but they're already making so many life changes they'll begrudgingly add one more. I was having difficulty in working and being able to help older people quit smoking. Then this year I had a perfect example to back up my thesis on change. A sixty-year-old salesman came to one of my groups. I noticed from the beginning that he talked only positively about quitting smoking. He was setting himself up for success. He had already read many of the books in the chapter on positive thinking that I had suggested smokers read before quitting. He had been "Practicing the art of making changes." He played tapes on positive thinking and reprogramming one's self for success while traveling in his car. When traveling and noticing a strong urge for cigarettes, he was willing to make big changes. That meant going out of his way to the next rest stop or restaurant where he would get a drink of water. The drink of water comforted him. And on the way to those places, he was willing to take his three deep breaths rather than dwelling on thoughts of cigarettes. He was going for success and he was already aware that success meant making changes. He was real encouragement for the people in the group who said, "If he can do it after smoking 45 years, we sure can do it, too." I've always believed that all of us are looking for true leaders, and he became one. He led the race and helped to bring others to the finish line.

What Are Some of the Changes That You May Have to Make?

If cigarettes are your "upper" in the morning to get moving, you'll need to make a change in the morning—a change that will avoid the temptation to have that first cigarette of the day. Are you willing to run-in-place instead? Or take a cold shower? Or go in and get a glass of ice water instead? These are all "uppers" or stimulants. Only a stimulant will replace a stimulant. Think up something special for yourself if you don't like my ideas. It takes about thirty to forty days for the new habit of "not smoking" to become a habit in itself. You won't have to take a cold shower for the rest of your life! This is not to be looked upon as a form of sadistic revenge on you for your smoking habit; it is just one of many ideas that may work for you. Personally, I was glad that my morning cigarette was one of the easier ones to give up so I didn't have a hard time substituting.

One of the most courageous changes I've heard about is the lady who wrapped her cigarettes in paper. She told herself that she could not have a cigarette unless she unwrapped the paper first and wrote down why she needed this cigarette and how she was feeling at the time. This is a good deterrent as you frequently lose the urge by the time you've gone through the ritual. But she also took her wrapped cigarettes and put them far out in her yard up in a tree. So she had to go outside, run down a hill, climb a tree, unwrap the cigarettes, and write about her needs. All of this just to have a smoke! This was incentive enough for her to quit. She made the changes that enabled her to become an ex-smoker. Some would say it was foolish, but at least she's not a smoking fool.

Maybe you are a RELAXATION SMOKER and when you take a break from work or from your chores, you take your "reward" with a cigarette. Or you take one as your "dessert" after a good meal. You'll have a make the change of finding something else that is as rewarding and as relaxing. A newspaper reporter in my group had always looked forward to her coffee break with a cigarette. She learned to take "deep breathing" breaks instead. Not as initially rewarding perhaps, but relaxing and healthy. Another woman took "running breaks" and learned to enjoy them. She was willing to do them until they became a more comfortable habit than a smoking break.

If you are a HANDLING SMOKER who needs something in your mouth and hands, you'll just have to switch to something else that keeps your hands and mouth busy. My sister quit smoking the same year I did. One of her major incentives was to provide a smoke-free living environment for her three-year-old twins. The first change she made was to start taking classes during the evening at a local junior college. She hadn't been in school for ten years. She also switched from cigarettes to shelling and devouring sunflower seeds. This kept both her hands and mouth busy and the seeds are a good source of protein and the B complex vitamins. She became so addicted to them she told the twins that someday she would probably have to go to a "SUN-FLOWER SEED WITHDRAWAL CLINIC." But it worked and she has been off cigarettes for over five years now. She is still making many changes. She found the courage to learn to drive a car. And she counsels others on how to stop smoking. She is of service to others instead of feeling sorry for herself about having a loss or change in her life. When we're together we sometimes have an urge for a cigarette at the same time if a stress situation comes up. But we can talk about it and laugh about it. It's no stronger than our urge for chocolate cake or Burt Reynolds. It's just the old trigger mechanism that was activated because a situation came up which we used to solve with cigarettes. The urge is but a memory of another time and way of reacting when we felt stress.

My favorite story concerns the girl in my group who had just moved from the South to Oregon. Talk about CHANGES! She was in a strange town, no longer teaching because she was raising a family, and she decided to quit smoking. She said she had to do things like run out to the washer in the garage, lift the lid, and yell obscenities into the washing machine while slamming down the lid to drown out the sound. And she doesn't even like to swear! But in a strange town with small chiidren underfoot who didn't go home when school was over, she had no one to talk to about her frustration of not being able to have a cigarette. So, she made changes. Now she no longer has to run out to the garage and talk to the washing machine. But she does talk a lot more, and she's proud of her accomplishment. She recently had her third baby. She has become a winner in the stop-smoking game.

There was another woman who was very worried about giving up cigarettes because she might gain weight. She learned to think positively and to make enough changes so she could quit smoking and not gain a pound. She wrote me recently to tell me—this brought me more joy than a bouquet of roses!

Another woman I know said the biggest change she made was deciding to go outside for her "after dinner" cigarette; this was her favorite cigarette and the last to be given up. It got colder and colder as winter drew on—she decided to stay inside, stay warm, and quit smoking. She also quit worrying about the five pounds she put on temporarily, and a year later is back to her original weight. She also felt that making the initial change to stop smoking led to many more changes in her life; she no longer fears change. She had smoked for twenty-five years. If you are a STRESS SMOKER like I was, the biggest change you'll have to make is starting to accept stress as natural and just do your best to deal with it. Don't waste your energy trying to change the world—change yourself. Since I've changed myself, the world doesn't seem half as bothersome!

As long as "change is the only constant," get used to it. It makes quitting smoking a lot easier. What is really important is to make a change that is good for you; make it something that you can look forward to doing. Some people go back to school, some take up scuba diving, some become volunteers in their community, some learn to knit or sew, some take up swimming or join the local health and fitness center. These can cost money, but you're going to have money to spend if you quit smoking. And you'll be spending it to live, rather than to self-destruct. Think what you've wanted to do since you were younger and never got around to doing. Do it now!!

If you can make the change to quit smoking, you have already changed your thinking process. Treat yourself to a dream—you're worth it!!

VII
On Being a Fool

"Would you allow the opinion of someone else to determine your future?"

An old adage goes, "Some people would rather DIE than make a FOOL out of themselves." What has this got to do with giving up smoking? When people choose to stop smoking, they are making an internal decision to live. They are choosing life over death at this time in their lives. This statement will anger some smokers; it took me three years off cigarettes to accept this idea. No one likes to be caught in the act of deliberately killing themselves. Most of us prefer it to be a private affair.

When smokers choose to quit smoking, they favor freedom over bondage. Any renewed freedom brings renewal of life. They are favoring self-control over self-degradation. This takes many changes, and it is much harder for some than for others. Even among hard-core smokers, there are varying degrees of dependency and need. It is often more difficult for those alone. Young mothers often say it is hardest for them because they have housework and children underfoot continually. To this I say, "No, at least you are needed and filling a role in society." The hardest smokers to deal with are those who have smoked over forty years or those who live alone. They must make the biggest changes. They have no one to share their pain and joy. Our society is still youth-oriented and those alone often feel unwanted and lacking a specific role.

So, let's invert that original statement to read, "Some people choose to make temporary FOOLS out of themselves in order to LIVE without cigarettes." The definition of a fool is "To jest; to make believe; to play." Doesn't sound too bad to me. Sounds like the kind of fun that only children and actors can have. Those of us who are successful ex-smokers all had to do some foolish-appearing things to divert us from the constant urge for cigarettes. Again, there are always the exceptions who breezed through the whole thing, but this book is not written for them. It is written for all those who have had bad experiences in the past when trying to quit smoking.

So, let's go back to being foolish. Even the Bible states, *"Whosoever shall not receive the kingdom of God as a little child, shall not enter therein"* (my emphasis).[1] The whole universe invites us to play as a child, but how long has it been since you've built a dream castle in the sand? How long since you've perched in a swing, pumped yourself up so high and felt the freedom of your feet off the ground? Or even gone to a movie and crunched on popcorn? Or played hide-and-seek with your children? Or jumped for a branch of a tree on a spring day? Only because you felt alive and thankful for the tree, and the sunshine, and your ability to jump?

There is one prerequisite for "real play." It is the same rule that small children follow. Since they are still in a "natural" state, I believe it to be a truthful and valid rule. You cannot be under the intoxication of booze, drugs, cigarettes, or other hallucinatory items. The true test is if you do

---

1. King James Version. Book of MARK. Chapter 10: Verse 15.

it just for the sake of wanting to do it, because you are still capable of <u>playing</u>. <u>Anyone</u> can do it while under the influence of stimulants. Which is what constitutes a true fool and has given the word "fool" a bad name.

EVERY CHILD IS BORN WITH THE ABILITY TO PLAY, but by age twelve most children have forgotten <u>how</u>! We become adults who take ourselves so seriously that we are continually disappointed when life keeps throwing "folly" our way. We don't even get the message that life is trying to throw to us. Of course, we must be responsible and earn our rent on planet Earth. And we must not hurt other fellow beings. When a person <u>thinks</u> they are playing by getting drunk, then crashes into an innocent family on a highway, they <u>hurt</u> others. Running, jumping, building sand castles, and experiencing glee does not <u>hurt</u> others. This is the difference between "real play" and "pretend play." What I'm talking about are <u>positive</u> child-like qualities that we all still possess. We've just filed them in our brain-computers under "Lost" . . . or "Forgotten."

How many of us spend the majority of our lives afraid that we might appear foolish? All we see are the problems and flaws of life. And the world <u>certainly</u> has flaws and problems if you choose to dwell on them.

So rather than look for the beauty and quality of life that still exist, we concentrate on the problems. Not solving them, just concentrating on them. And because concentrating on them has never been the answer, we feel lonely and uncomfortable with ourselves and others around us. Rather than <u>give</u> a little to solve the problems as our personal contribution to the gift of life, we let the problems overwhelm us. We start overdrinking, smoking, overeating, denying our spirutal needs, spacing out, and soaking in all the negativity we can find. It still feels so terrible that we get further out of touch with ourselves by escaping <u>further</u> into these substitutes. We think we now fit into society, but it still doesn't feel good.

When you decide to quit smoking, you'll again fit into your own personal universe, but you may not feel so comfortable in society. You may find it awkward with nothing in your hands and you can't pose with your cigarette. So you may learn to become a little foolish and wad up paper napkins at parties and in restaurants. You won't feel this need at home alone because there is no one to impress but yourself, and you already impressed yourself when you quit smoking. Or you may have a terrible oral need to smoke while out among people. Carry a cut-in-half straw for this purpose. You'll put it in your mouth and "puff" on it, and it will keep your hands busy at the same time. You may look like a fool to some people, but at least you'll know you aren't a "smoking fool."

For awhile it may seem difficult to fit back into society without your cigarettes, but the greatest part is that you'll "fit" back into yourself, and that feels good. Some people burst into tears or experience anger for no apparent reason during the withdrawal period from nicotine. Society considers this social unacceptable. And perhaps foolish. But the crying and anger bit only lasts a few days. Just a <u>few days</u> out of your life you may appear foolish to some people. But you will not appear so to those who know what you are <u>accomplishing</u> by giving up cigarettes. You will not appear foolish to wise and understanding people. You would probably appear more foolish if you gave in to your self-consciousness and started smoking again. And <u>who</u> wants to go through withdrawal over and over again?

When people asked me what I was doing with the straw in my mouth, I said, "<u>I'm smoking a straw</u>." I may have looked foolish to some "perfect people," but I looked pretty good to myself and I am the only one who will be present for the Final Judgment. I'd feel even more foolish if I had to give in to cigarettes again, and I couldn't have written this book because I would have cared more what others thought than what I thought of myself.

When I mention in my groups that some people might even want to use baby pacifiers temporarily while alone at home or alone in the car, embarrassment, laughter, and then silence occur. But many smokers when they really quit have mentioned that when they see babies with pacifiers, they get terrible urges to pull them out of their mouths. They feel foolish about these feelings, but they share them with others, deal with them, accept them, and continue to stay off cigarettes. This is all that counts.

Many women feel like fools if they gain an ounce after they quit smoking. They allow the opinions of husbands, friends, and lovers to influence them negatively. But if they really want to quit smoking, they put up with this temporary nuisance. They tackle the cigarette habit first, then they get back to the weight. They learn what really being foolish is when they see other women their age ruining their looks and natural glow by continuing to smoke. I knew I'd always feel like the biggest fool in the world if I kept smoking and someday had to tell my daughters or grandchildren that I couldn't live to see them grow up because I chose nicotine over them.

Only a fool like I was could ever believe that the tobacco industry cares about us as living human beings. They laugh all the way to the bank after deluding us that we'll be sensuous, cool, intelligent, and free to make the choice to smoke. We may be free to start smoking, but we're not nearly as free to quit. We become addicts—which is exactly what the tobacco industry counts on. I was made a fool by cigarettes, and I'll show them for what they really are.

You may feel foolish when you need to take your three deep breaths instead of reaching for a cigarette. Someone may laugh. Just keep remembering that those who laugh will not be there when you get lung cancer. Only you will be there. When you feel panic in a stress situation, you may have to run in place or suck on a straw to distract yourself temporarily. What this all means is that you value your self-opinion more than the opinion of those who may ridicule you or laugh at you. Most who laugh and ridicule will be smokers. You're going up to a higher level in life, and the smokers will be left in the basement. They'll try and get you to stay. Forgive them for that. It's lonely in the basement.

IT IS YOUR MIND, YOUR BODY, AND YOUR CHOICE. Treasure the choice to stop smoking. Make it a desire rather than a deprivation. When someone puts you down for needing substitutes or acting temporarily "crazy" or foolish, give the problem back to them. Ask them, "Now why did you feel the need to say that?" Say it inquisitively and kindly. Give the problem back to them; it wasn't yours in the first place.

And most of all FORGIVE YOUR FRIENDS who are threatened by the change you are making in your life. *"Change is the only constant," but it is frightening to many people.* They fear it rather than see the chance to grow with it. It causes "waves" in everyday routine, so be patient with friends, family, and co-workers who feel insecure with the new you.

Each person is very individual in the way that they will choose to quit smoking. Robert Blake, who plays "Baretta" on television, has not smoked for ten years, but he keeps an unlit cigarette in his mouth for old times' sake. Some would say he is foolish for not letting cigarettes go completely from his life, but I admire him. He quit smoking. He chose good health. He is an excellent physical specimen for a man approaching fifty years of age. He wouldn't be if he were still smoking. Personally, I could not have an unlit cigarette in my mouth without wanting to devour it! But for Blake, it works!

Start finding out now what works for you. Some of you will be surprised to find that the fear of quitting is more more frightening than the actual experience. You won't even need to appear foolish. To the rest of us, *"There is no fool like a happy fool."*

VIII
Weight Control

"FAT FEAR" is a major reason many smokers continue to smoke. Women in particular mention that they smoke to keep their weight down. How unfortunate that "fat fear" has been around so long everyone chooses to believe that they will become obese if they quit smoking. There are people who gained many pounds when they quit smoking, but they didn't know better. Or they might have been told so many times they would become fat, they began to believe it. Then, after they had begun to believe it, they began to live it. They fulfilled the prophecy that others designed for them.

Some people consider it socially unacceptable to be a smoker. Others consider it socially unacceptable to be obese. The truth is probably neither is socially acceptable in our society. We are a weight-conscious, health-conscious nation. Medical science tells us it would take at least fifty to seventy-five pounds of extra weight to do the same damage to your heart that smoking does. The big fear is of lung cancer, but smoking remains the number one factor in heart disease and the "sudden death syndrome" and actually damages your heart more than your lungs.

But back to the positive side of this issue. You do not want to gain a lot of weight when you quit smoking and you do not have to gain any weight when you quit smoking. It is your choice. After the initial nervousness of withdrawal is over, you will become more relaxed and easygoing, and your metabolism will slow down to normal. This may add five pounds or so on some people. Without that nervous, high-gear feeling, you may tend to put on weight. You may keep the five pounds or you may lose it as your body metabolism adjusts back to being a non-smoker. If you choose not to keep the five pounds, just increase your energy output in the form of exercise: walking, swimming, jogging—or whatever your physician suggests as acceptable for your particular body.

If you keep telling yourself that you are going to gain weight when you quit smoking, you probably will gain weight. If you repeat anything to yourself long enough, your subconscious will believe it and carry out those orders for you. Why not brainwash yourself positively into believing you will remain thin? "REPETITION REINFORCES BELIEF." So repeat only those thoughts that will keep you thin. Repeat to yourself: "I am a thin ex-smoker." You will eventually begin to believe it; only then will you act it out by eating less food. This thought process will become a part of you. Try it—it only works if you USE it.

You will always have well-intentioned friends who tell you that you will become fat if you stop smoking. Whenever they do this, quietly repeat the positive phrase to yourself to counteract their negative phrases.

You've also probably heard the expression, "Garbage in, garbage out." This refers to the fact that if you put garbage into a computer, garbage comes out. The same is true for your brain. If you fill it with garbage, you have garbage coming out. Your brain processes and assimilates whatever you put into it. Why put in negative thoughts about becoming fat? I heard a beautiful actress interviewed once on a talk show. Someone asked her if she could ever visualize herself as fat someday. She replied with confidence, *"No, I will never be fat. I think thin."* As simple as that! She is a product of her thinking. She is practicing the technique, perhaps, unconsciously, of seeing herself only as a thin person. She gets results from thinking thin. She doesn't use fad diets that are only temporary and damaging to the body. She uses her brain to stay thin. It is your brain that keeps you from opening the refrigerator door. Your hands won't open the door unless ordered by your brain to do so.

There are many examples of beautiful women who don't do harmful things to stay thin. They all seem to have the same positive thought processes for taking care of their bodies. They eat healthy, balanced meals consisting of very little white flour and white sugar products. They drink lots of water, choose nutritious snacks, and their main meat dishes consist of fish and chicken. Common sense is what they put into their computers and common sense eating habits come out of their computers. The products are healthy, thin bodies. Some of these women who choose to eat wisely are Crystal Gayle, Marie Osmond, Susan Anton, Jacklyn Smith, Cheryl Tiegs, Farrah Fawcett, Phyllis George, Christina Ferrare, Gloria Vanderbilt, Ann Landers, Jane Fonda, Cher, Gloria Swanson, and the list goes on and on. They may all splurge occasionally due to the humanness they all possess, but there's no doubt they do a lot of positive talking to themselves to get back on the wagon to weight control . . . AND good health.

If you are already overweight before you quit smoking, start visualizing yourself as you would like to be. Paste pictures of thin, healthy women on your refrigerator so your brain gets the message that you want to be thin. Maybe you'll close the refrigerator and decide you don't need that ice cream! Yes, this will take work—there is no magic in becoming successful. It can be simple, but it takes a lifetime commitment to your new way of thinking. You'll have to make changes in your life. You'll have to start thinking positively about yourself and feel worthy of your goal.

Enclosed you will find a sheet with some food substitutes for cigarettes. CHOOSE WHAT APPEALS TO YOU. . . . Concentrate on the foods that are high in vitamin B complex and vitamin C. These are your stress vitamins and are depleted daily because they are water-soluble. Notice that the fourth column of the food substitute list has both the words CALORIE and ENERGY. In nutritional terms, they are interchangeable; the food industry uses this to their advantage. The definition of a calorie is: "The quantity of heat required to raise the temperature of one gram of water one degree centigrade." Physically speaking, it means "the quantity of food capable of producing such a unit of energy." And here is where the advertising geniuses proceed to treat us as fools. They know when we are tired, depressed, or bored, we will grab for a food labeled "HIGH IN ENERGY" or "FULL OF ENERGY." We crave ENERGY and what we often get instead is just CALORIES with no nutritional value whatsoever. The food labels are often actually stating, "High in CALORIES," "Full of CALORIES," but we fall for it because we are tired or vulnerable. Advertisers know we are afraid of the word CALORIES but impressed with the word ENERGY. So start reading the labels before you buy. If one of the first ingredients listed is sugar, forget it!! You get plenty of natural sugar in fruits, vegetables, milk products, and breads and cereals. Refined sugar is "the king of empty foods"—it gives you nothing but calories. They just call it energy to confuse us!

If you are truly concerned about your weight, YOU WILL EDUCATE YOURSELF! We cannot depend on the food industry to do this for us. In fact, David Rueben, M.D., advises in his book, *Everything You Always Wanted to Know About Nutrition: "Don't buy food advertised on* *television. One minute of advertising costs from $100,000.00 to $200,000.00."* He also says: "You can't EAT the T.V. ads, so don't PAY for them . . . food processors can afford only to advertise foods that have no real food value—most are artificially flavored and colored."[1]

Whenever I crave ENERGY, I've learned to test my ENERGY STORAGE. It's called the "pinch test." Whenever I want to overeat to get more energy, I just pinch my excess ENERGY STORAGE and remind myself that I am still carrying plenty of <u>reserve</u> CALORIES or ENERGY upon my very being.

Start really taking note of what foods are nutritional. Stop worrying so much about the calories, and start concentrating on getting enough wholesome nutrition. If you eat wholesome, nutritious meals, you won't be so tempted to cheat. If apple juice satisfies your sweet tooth, have one glass a day, but generally stick to the more nutritious juices like tomato, vegetable, and grapefruit. Keep sugarless gum and mints handy at all times.

Copy the substitute snack list, stick it on your refrigerator, and become knowledgeable about what you put into your body. Try to eliminate any foods which contain white sugar and white flour. Stick with the whole wheat grains and bread products. People are too worried about not having enough energy if they cut down on foods filled with white sugar. You <u>don't</u> need white sugar for energy. <u>You need carbohydrates</u>. An orange is a natural way of obtaining carbohydrates for energy. A piece of whole wheat bread or a plate of brown rice is high-energy food. They convert to simple sugar in the body just as white sugar does, but they <u>also</u> contain minerals and vitamins needed for good health and tissue maintenance and repair. <u>White sugar has none of these qualities</u>—only calories and simple carbohydrates. Why waste your money and time on "empty foods"? And why waste your body energy digesting and metabolizing them? You wouldn't pay good money to put "empty fuel" into your car. <u>Why put it into your body</u>? Stick to the nutritious foods that will give you energy, nutrients, and a body that doesn't resemble the "Pillsbury Dough Boy." Remember—garbage in, garbage out. Who wants a body that looks like garbage? "We are what we eat." I've often said that I'd rather look like a proud carrot stick than a pasty doughnut. I have been fat. I didn't like being fat. I use the same techniques to stay slender that I used to stop smoking. After all, we smoke, overeat, and overdrink for many of the same reasons, so why not use the same techniques to quit them?

KEEP YOUR FOOD SUBSTITUTES HANDY AT ALL TIMES DURING THE WITHDRAWAL PERIOD. Keep your plastic straws that you cut in half available, too. Plan to have them in your car and work areas, at home, etc. They may be just enough distraction at a critical time to be the difference between whether you make it or not. It's really not the big things that decide—it's the thirty to sixty little habitual things called "urges" that pop up daily.

Keep lots of carrots, celery, sugarless gum and mints handy. It takes about as many calories to consume them as they contain, so they are often called "free foods." <u>Protein snacks are good</u>. They come in the form of peanuts, sunflower seeds, jerky, cheese, etc. Just remember, however, to eat them in <u>small</u> amounts as they contain many calories in large amounts, as well as salt and fat. <u>Think</u> little, <u>eat</u> little, and <u>be</u> little. You really won't be obsessed with food for very long anyway. We're just talking about the first few weeks that the body is confused and feeling empty. The urge for food will diminish. You'll find other satisfactory substitutes and will become an example of a happy, slim, and healthy ex-smoker. Read some well-balanced books on nutrition. Stay away from the myths of dieting and start educating yourself on the facts of sensible eating that will help to ensure you a lifetime of looking and feeling good. Start by reading some of the books in Recommended Reading in the back of this book.

1. Reuben, David, M.D. *Everything You Always Wanted To Know About Nutrition.* New York: Avon Books, 1978.

28.4 grams = one ounce
(30 grams = one ounce
 for practical purposes)

SUBSTITUTE SNACK FOODS — CALORIC AND NUTRITIVE VALUES*

FOOD	WGT. Gram	APPROXIMATE MEASURE	ENERGY Calories	PROTEIN Gram	FAT Gram	TOTAL CARBO-HYDRATE Gram	WATER Gram	CALCIUM Mg.	IRON Mg.	VITA-MIN A I.U.	THIA-MIN (B1) Mg.	RIBO-FLAVIN (B2) Mg.	NIACIN (B3) Mg.	VITA-MIN C Mg.
Peach, raw	115	1 medium	45	.7	.1	11	103	10	.6	1530	.02	.06	1.2	0
Orange juice (fresh/canned)	185	6 ounces	80	1.0	.4	19	163	20	.4	370	.17	.06	.7	93
Tomato Juice	180	6 ounces	35	1.5	.2	8	169	13	1.6	1440	.09	.05	1.4	29
Vegetable Cock-tail, V-8	180	6 ounces	35	1.0	-	8	171	22	.40	1750	.06	.04	1.2	27
Sunflower Seeds (kernels/shelled)	30	1 ounce	110	4.3	9.0	4	4.8	21	1.2	9	.35	.04	.9	tr.
Bread, whole-wheat	23	1 slice	55	2.5	.7	11	8	23	.5	tr.	.06	.03	.7	tr.
Peanuts, shelled/roasted	15	15-20 nuts	90	4.0	8.0	3	tr.	11	.3	-	.05	.02	2.6	-
Carrots	50	1 carrot	20	.6	.1	5	44	19	.4	5500	.03	.03	.3	4
Popcorn (w/small amt. oil & salt)	15	1 cup	60	2.0	3.0	9	1	1	.3	-	-	.01	.3	0
Hard Candy/Sucker	30	1 ounce	115	-	.3	29	.4	6	.6	-	-	-	-	-
Yogurt (low-fat)	246	1 cup	125	8.5	4.0	13	219	295	tr.	170	.10	.44	.2	2
Recommended Daily Allowance (RDA) for Adults and projected dietary goals for U.S. of carbohydrates, fats and proteins				PROTEIN 12% of Total Diet	FAT 30% of Total Diet	CARBOHYDRATE 58% Total Diet (only 10% from refined products--the rest to be complex (starchy) and naturally occurring, such as in fruit)		CALCIUM 800 mg.	IRON 18 mg	VIT.A 5,000 I.U.	B1 1.5 mg.	B2 1.7 mg.	B3 20 mg.	VIT.C 60 mg.

Approximate amount of caffeine in drinks and chocolate can vary greatly with strength and amount used --

Coffee	85 mg./6 oz. coffee	Chocolate 65 mg./1 oz.
Black Tea	50 mg./6 oz. black tea	Coke & Soft Drinks w/caffeine 30-65 mg./12 oz.
Green Tea	30 mg./6 oz. green tea	
Cocoa	30 mg./6 oz.	

*Source: Adapted from *Agriculture Handbook #8*, USDA.

65

How Much of Your Food Is Fat?

Calories from fat in common foods

75% of calories	mayonnaise avocado cream cheese peanut butter French Dressing	bacon peanuts sunflower seeds Blue Cheese Dressing Italian Dressing	sausage olives almonds
50 to 75% of calories	eggs pork chops T-bone steak American cheese regular hamburger	bologna potato chips batter fried fish chocolate candy bar Cheddar & other natural cheeses	ice cream Big Mac Swiss cheese
30 to 50% of calories	fried chicken French fries biscuits creamed cottage cheese pancakes trimmed meats	doughnuts hash browns muffins Oreo cookies cake with icing	cream soup granola whole milk 2% milk ham salmon
15 to 30% of calories	buttermilk low-fat yogurt cornbread soft rolls & buns low-fat cottage cheese light meat of chicken or turkey without skin	flour tortillas oatmeal veal beef round	oysters liver crab clams
less than 15% of calories	fresh fruits vegetables pickles breads hot-air popcorn corn tortillas water-pack tuna skim milk cheeses	cod juices sauerkraut noodles dry beans, peas angel food cake broth soups	halibut shrimp scallops cereals skim milk spaghetti

*Nutrition Workshop Information, reprinted by permission of Susan B. Deeming, Ph.D., R.D.

Nutrition in the Fast Lane*

Good nutrition is vital for top performance! Both the competitive athlete and the individual involved in a fitness program benefit from good nutrition but there is no MAGIC involved.

A diet which supplies enough, but not too much, carbohydrate, fat, protein, vitamins, minerals and water is of key importance to all athletes.

CARBOHYDRATE:
- provides energy for body processes.
- is the preferred fuel for muscles.
- is the most economical source of energy.

FAT:
- supplies the essential fatty acid.
- provides fat soluble vitamins.
- is a concentrated source of energy. It has twice the calories of carbohydrate or protein.

PROTEIN:
- is necessary for growth, repair, and maintenance of body tissues.
- is necessary for the production of hormones, enzymes and antibodies.
- Overconsumption may cause stress on the liver and kidneys.
- Overconsumption does not build extra muscle or give an athlete an advantage.

VITAMINS AND MINERALS:
- Rely on a variety of foods to supply the necessary vitamins and minerals.
- Supplements are unnecessary.
- Mega-doses may interfere with the use of other nutrients.
- Iron deficiency may affect performance because not enough oxygen is carried to muscles to allow their efficient use. Women and growing children may lack enough iron in their diets.

WATER:
- is necessary for all body processes.
- prevents dehydration during strenuous exercise and warm weather.
- can be provided by diluted fruit juice. Athletic beverages are not needed.

*Margaret J. Lewis, R.D., Extension Nutrition Specialist, Oregon State University, January 1984

EXERCISE AND ENERGY USE

- Glucose is the primary fuel source for high-intensity, short-duration exercise.
- When exercise continues for five minutes or longer, both glucose and fat are used for fuel.
- If exercise continues, fat becomes the major fuel for muscles.
- Endurance events use the glycogen stored in muscles and the liver.
- Carbohydrate loading is a dietary manipulation to increase muscle and liver glycogen stores. The larger these stores are, the longer fatigue may be avoided.

  CAUTION: There are unpleasant side effects—fatigue, nausea, irritability, water retention and weight gain. Exercise during depletion may cause heart beat irregularities.

  Carbohydrate loading should be used ONLY by endurance athletes under the supervision of an expert.

- High protein foods are not the best for a pre-game meal; they take longer to digest than carbohydrates and may cause stomach upsets.

THE CALORIE COST OF ACTIVITIES

Activity Level	Calories Used Per Minute
Sleeping	1
Very light exercise: Office work, drinking, reading, watching TV, studying, telephoning, typing	2
Light exercise: Housework, shopping, golf, volleyball, walking slowly, fishing, riding horseback at a walk	2–5
Moderate exercise: Walking fast, playing tennis, gardening, skiing downhill, bicycling slowly, hiking, dancing slowly, swimming leisurely, playing baseball.	5–7
Heavy exercise: Playing basketball, weight lifting, playing football, running, cross-country skiing, bicycle racing, horseback riding at a gallop.	7–12

RECOMMENDATIONS FOR EATING

- Choose a variety of foods from the basic food groups that will meet your caloric needs.
- Avoid protein supplements, vitamin or mineral supplements, or foods or beverages that promise special advantages to the athlete.
- Choose a pregame meal that is high in carbohydrate and moderate in protein and fat.
- Drink plenty of water before, during and after exercise.

THE SECRET OF GOOD PHYSICAL PERFORMANCE IS HARD TRAINING, NATURAL TALENT, MOTIVATION AND GOOD NUTRITION.

None of these books is a book on magic—only on the <u>potential</u> for success. They visualize the ability of every person to achieve his or her own degree of success through positive thinking. They will give you techniques and tools to use that will enable you to think of yourself not only as an ex-smoker, but a thin ex-smoker.

<u>Most important of all</u>, start thinking of yourself as lucky and fortunate to be giving up cigarettes. YOUR ATTITUDE IS THE MOST IMPORTANT ASSET you have going for you. Keep a positive attitude and you'll keep your body trim!

Nutritious Foods to Help You Maintain Your Weight When Quitting Smoking

SUNFLOWER SEEDS

They stimulate the adrenal glands as nicotine did, which in turn lifts and stimulates us. The seeds contain oils which are calming. They are heavy in the B complex vitamins that help rebuild the nervous system. They are an excellent source of protein. They keep the hands and mouth very busy if you buy them in the shells. If you buy them unshelled, it is best to buy them raw . . . keep a handful of them handy at work, home, in the purse, pockets, car.
<u>CALORIES: Approximately 120 per ounce.</u>

POPCORN

A good source of complex carbohydrate, some protein, Vitamin A, traces of Iron, Vitamins B-2 and B-3, and Fat. This is an excellent substitute if chewed slowly for better absorption. You can make it ahead of time and take it with you to work, or have handy in the car. It is a good "anger" food as you get "crunching satisfaction" from eating it.
<u>CALORIES: Approximately 50 calories/cup air popped; 150 calories/cup with butter.</u> (Note: Popcorn is <u>not</u> fattening; it's what you put <u>on</u> it!!)

CARROTS

They are good substitutes for handling your thoughts and keeping them diverted from smoking by being able to "crunch." They are an excellent source of Vitamin A which builds strong membranes for the respiratory system (lungs), and for formation of mucosa (or <u>internal</u> skin). They contain Protein, Carbohydrate, Calcium, traces of Iron, Vitamins B-1, B-2, B-3 and Vitamin C.
<u>CALORIES: One carrot is only 20–25 calories.</u>

LOW-FAT YOGURT

Excellent source of Protein, Calcium, and good sources of Vitamin A, Carbohydrate, and Fat. Traces of Vitamins B-1, B-2, B-3, and Vitamin C. Try this instead of ice cream or other high sugar desserts. If you don't like it plain, add your own honey, granola, mixed fruit, or vanilla.
<u>CALORIES: Approximately 120–150 calories per cup.</u>

PEANUTS

Excellent source of Protein, Fat, Carbohydrate, Calcium, Vitamins B-1, B-2, and Iron. A small amount is satisfying.
<u>CALORIES: Approximately 100 calories per 10–15 nuts.</u>

NOTE: The above foods are not "empty foods" (foods which contain calories but no nutritional values). They are nutritional, but <u>moderation</u> is still the key because if eaten in large quantities (except carrots), you will be taking in too many calories and will gain unnecessary pounds which can tempt you back to smoking. Remember that potatoes, bread, and popcorn are not fattening foods—it's the excess butter, jam, and gravies we put on them. When in doubt, <u>"SMOKE" A STRAW OR CHEW A CARROT!!!</u>

Base/Alkaline Foods That Ease Withdrawal

The main purpose in quitting smoking is to get the nicotine out of the bloodstream within 2–4 days so the actual physiological withdrawal is over and you can get on with the emotional and intellectual withdrawal. Yet, you do not want to flush it out so quickly that withdrawal is intense enough to cancel all memory traces of ever having wanted to quit smoking.

Many university researchers have theorized that because nicotine is such an incredibly strong base substance, if too many acid-forming foods are taken into the body, the nicotine would be flushed out so quickly, <u>more</u> base substance—or nicotine—would be required to replace it. So why not merely <u>replace</u> some of the lost base substance/nicotine with base-forming foods—the more alkaline/base in the smoker's body, the less a smoker would theoretically need to smoke, because the urge is satisfied by base-forming foods. That may be a simplified explanation to a complicated theory, but this is not a chemistry book. However, it <u>does</u> work for those who are willing to try it, and every trick YOU are willing to try will put you just that much closer to success.*

Foods are classified as acid-forming or base-forming elements left after the food is digested or oxidized in the body. You may argue that some of the foods are really "acidic foods." Yes, they are acid-foods <u>outside</u> the body before we eat them, but their chemical make-up changes after they are eaten or digested—they are base/alkaline forming <u>inside</u> the body. The acid-forming foods are usually high in protein which contain sulphur and phosphorus—like meat and eggs. The base-forming foods are usually fruits, vegetables, milk and nuts. The foods on the top of the list are more effective than the foods at the bottom of the list—they decline in effectiveness as we go down the list:**

1) Molasses *(2 tsp.)*	6) Carrot	11) Strawberries
2) Raisins	7) Celery	12) Mushrooms
3) Figs	8) Grapefruit	13) Apples
4) Spinach, Beet Greens	9) Sweet potatoes	14) Milk
5) Almonds	10) Tomatoes	15) Onion

Exercise and Smoking

Engaging in physical activity is an effective method in countering smoking urges. Short exercise breaks—a brisk five-minute walk, a dive in the pool, skipping rope 50 times—are useful as immediate substitutes when you feel a strong craving to smoke. As a long-term alternative to smoking, a sensible and suitable aerobic exercise program can be the "magic" that keeps you

---

*Caution: Do not eat <u>only</u> these foods; just include them in your normal diet. If your physician has you on a special diet because of a medical condition, please consult with him/her first.

**The foods listed above were adapted from a chart appearing in *Hawk's Physiological Chemistry* (McGraw-Hill, Inc., New York), 1965.

permanently off cigarettes. By using your body, you will find you have more energy, an enhanced sense of well-being, and a calmer, more relaxed attitude towards the daily frustrations and pressures of life.

Since most smokers in the early stages of quitting would give anything to feel calm, relaxed or even energetic, it's only natural that exercise is a highly recommended antidote during smoking cessation.

Too busy to exercise? Aerobic programs—running, walking, swimming, cycling, skipping rope—can be accomplished in a minimum of 12–15 minutes four times a week. Remember, you burn up 1–2 hours a day just smoking, not to mention time spent in "quick" trips to the store for cigarettes, emptying and cleaning ash trays, and extra smoke breaks during the work day.

What is aerobic exercise? An aerobic exercise is one which

1. is steady and non-stop,
2. lasts a minimum of 12–15 minutes,
3. maintains your heart rate at 65–80% of the maximum,
4. should be done a minimum of four days per week, and
5. provides physical and mental benefits.

Many people enthusiastically begin exercise programs only to give up after a short period of time. This happens primarily because people tend to over-exercise, which can lead to injury and frustration; or they choose an unsuitable type of exercise. A gentle, gradual approach to beginning a program is vital. A fairly sedentary person can change into a fit, active being—but not overnight! And if you despise getting your hair wet, swimming probably isn't your "magic."

Choose a type of exercise that appeals to you; one that fits into your life without great difficulty or sacrifice. Commit yourself to a three-month trial period. Proceed slowly and cautiously—as time goes by the exercise program will become a pleasant part of your daily routine. As a fit, healthy person, the idea of having "just one cigarette" will be far less tempting.

Useful references for getting started in aerobics:

FIT OR FAT? by Covert Baily. Houghton Mifflin Co., 1977.
    Common sense approach to aerobics; clear and concise.

THE NEW AEROBICS by Kenneth Cooper, M.D. Bantam Books, 1970.

Courtesy of Merrie Ziady, Health Educator
Portland, Oregon

"Hmmmmmm-you can't quit smoking and your lungs have had it, so step over to window number one and get yourself a _good_ used pair."

IX

For Physicians Only

"Men do not usually die—they kill themselves."—Michel de Montaigne

Do you know that EIGHTY PERCENT of smokers interviewed said that they would stop smoking if their doctors insisted? This lays a heavy burden of responsibility on you. Actually, I'm impressed with the trend of medicine where doctors are now teaching patients to <u>also</u> be responsible for their own health. Let's assume they have the intelligence to be responsible.

But there still seems to be the child in us who wants the doctor to say, "You must stop smoking," or "You must lose weight," or "You must stop drinking so heavily." Apparently patients still want the <u>initial</u> order given. Then they can follow through on their own in accomplishing the goal. Of course many need referrals to agencies, weight loss programs, Alcoholics Anonymous, etc. But the responsibility is felt to carry out the order given by the doctor. And the tone of the voice must mean business. Yes, the child in us all cries out for those whom we respect to point the way. Many ex-smokers are alive only because their doctors had the COURAGE to tell them to quit smoking.

So many of the people I have seen in my groups are only there because their doctors insisted. Of course they must do it for themselves, but the insistence by their doctors gave them the courage to ask for help. They are now <u>ex-smokers</u> because they want to continue feeling healthy and responsible for their own lives.

I've heard so many people in the past complain, "All a doctor does about my weight is hand me a 1200 calorie diet sheet." This is no longer true. Doctors are becoming more knowledgeable about nutrition and are talking to their patients about their weight. When doctors aren't comfortable doing this, they are referring their patients to Weight Watchers, diet services, etc. The same goes for smoking. You just can't nonchalantly tell your patients to stop smoking. <u>Be sure you know the stop-smoking services your community has to offer.</u> Personally, I like my method of positive reinforcement and visualization techniques, but if hypnosis, aversion therapy, or acupuncture appeals more to the patient, let them try it. Each patient smokes <u>differently</u> and will want different modes of therapy to help them stop smoking.

THERE ARE MANY RELIABLE ORGANIZATIONS THAT OFFER PLANS TO QUIT SMOKING, such as The Lung Association, the Heart Association, the American Cancer Society, Seventh Day Adventists, or the local hospital group plan such as I am now affiliated with. Know the phone numbers of these organizations. Have your receptionist or nurse keep an active file with these groups and plans listed. If the patient complains about the <u>costs</u> of some of these plans, remind them that it takes over $400.00 a year to support their smoking habit. If they say they don't have time to go for help, remind them it takes at least 365 hours a year to smoke. This includes lighting the cigarettes, going to the store to get them, running around to find them, and the actual act of smoking. Remind them it takes <u>strength</u> to ask for help.

If the patients have family members who nag continually to you about their smoking, remind them that nagging doesn't work. If it did, there would be "nagging clinics" springing up all over the nation.

I also believe that unless you set an example yourself for your patients, the suggestions you give will only be "swallowed," never "digested." They will probably secretly just continue their destructive habit. If you deceive them, they will deceive you. <u>This brings us to the subject of smoking doctors</u>. Though setting an example and insisting that the patient quit smoking is always the most effective method, the fact remains that some physicians are still smoking. They don't intend to see their retirement years. Or, if they are lucky, they will see them, but the quality of life will be pitiful. I've worked for doctors and I respect the nature and burden of their profession; the stress and responsibilities are tremendous, but it does not help you or your patients if you continue to smoke yourself and contract lung disease, heart disease, etc. long before retirement. You are entitled to a long and healthy retirement.

I do not see the universe sending out signals of wisdom that encourage you to continue your smoking habit. You are responding to stress situations and habit, the same as your patients who smoke respond to stress situations and habit. We all prefer to think that our professions are more stressful and trying than another's, but the point is we had freedom to choose our profession and the stress it entails. When we have stressful occupations, why add the stress of smoking so we now have <u>two</u> stressful situations? The greatest shock for all of us who have been off cigarettes for the initial nervous withdrawal period is that we are more relaxed and tranquil after the first month <u>without them</u>. We have been conned into believing that cigarettes relax us when, in reality, they are stimulants and keep our motors idling at a nervous high.

Yes, it would take time out of your life to quit smoking. Take the ten to fifteen hours it takes in a group situation to quit. To comfortably let the smoking habit go, you first have to understand it. You owe it to yourself, and in exchange you'll receive many more years of quality life. You'll be able to see that retirement that you are entitled to. <u>You'll live to see your grandchildren, and set healthy examples for your own children and grandchildren</u>. Seems like a fair exchange—take time and a few miserable days of withdrawal and you'll add years to your life. Pretend you're going through the twenty-four hour flu; nothing makes it better but time. And just when we pray to die to escape the misery, the flu breaks. And withdrawal periods break, and the sun shines on our self-control again.

Take these same goal-achieving strengths that took you through medical school and "re-light" them when you decide to quit "lighting up."

The Myths and Realities of Cigarette Smoking

MYTH ....
Smokers are outdoor types
They can be seen riding horses,
Running in meadows,
Frolicking in forests,
And climbing big mountains.

REALITY ....
Smokers are outdoors by <u>request</u>,
Their horses are seen looking for
"No Smoking" sections in the meadows,
They <u>burn</u> down the forests,
And they can be seen climbing the <u>walls</u>
if they can't find a cigarette.

MYTH ....
Smokers are the liberated type,
They are busy catching planes,
They are very popular,
And they are always successful.

REALITY ....
To be liberated is to be free.
What is <u>free</u> about an addiction?
Smokers <u>catch</u> planes & emphysema.
They <u>are</u> popular with morticians.
And they <u>are</u> successful when it
comes to shortening lifespans.

MYTH ....
Smoking is very sensuous ....

REALITY ....
What is sensuous about "ashtray
breath," stained teeth, and pre-
maturely wrinkled faces?

MYTH ....
The tobacco industry really <u>cares</u>
about you as a person ....

REALITY ....
The tobacco industry <u>cares</u> about
your becoming <u>addicted</u>, but don't
call on them for help. They'll
put you on HOLD....<u>forever</u>!

L. BRYSON © 1980

A Short Smoking Story

Once upon a time there were two teenage girls who dreamed about becoming GLAMOROUS, SENSUOUS, and POPULAR. . . . Cigarette advertising made it appear that perhaps smoking cigarettes would make all their dreams come true. . . .

So, at age sixteen, Linda and Barbara forced their little sisters to take pictures of them posing for their first smoking experience. . . .

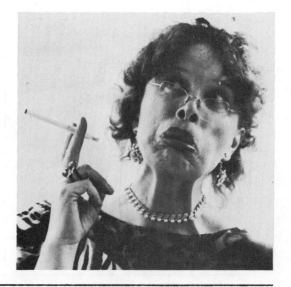

And . . . they didn't end up looking glamorous. But . . . they persisted, practiced, and pretended. Until something finally happened—they became *VERY ADDICTED!!!*

THE END ?

X

To Young Adults Only

"Don't let cigarettes become such a part of you that you can't part with them."—L.B.

You've already been told in school what smoking does to your lungs, heart, and circulation, so I'm not going to get into the technical and physical aspects of smoking. What I want to talk about are the MENTAL ASPECTS of smoking on young people.

My first qualification for talking about this is the fact that I started smoking when I was sixteen years old. Not only was it THE thing to be doing, but it also made my father crazy. Neither of my parents smoked. My dad said "he didn't want anything slowing him down." And at age 69, he is still going strong. Because my parents didn't smoke, I didn't see any of the negative aspects of smoking, like dirty ashtrays, holes in clothes and furniture, morning cough, frequent colds and bronchitis. All I saw were my friends smoking and the advertisements that guaranteed we'd be sensuous, popular and cool.

In fact, I must have really been impressed with the advertisements because I found an old snapshot that a friend took of me and my girlfriend having our first cigarette. At that time, I believed I looked beautiful smoking. When I found the picture twenty years later, I was embarrassed for myself. Looking at this picture I don't see beauty, sensuousness, or popularity. I see the first cigarette that was the beginning of an addictive habit that eventually took away my personal freedom. And I also see insecurity, defiance, and rebellion. I am aware that all young people experience these feelings to some degree or another; some just find better ways of dealing with them. Somehow they have the awareness that smoking will not solve these problems, that smoking only postpones the problems.

So as my problems built up, I smoked rather than talk about them. I pretended that smoking helped the problems go away, but the joke was on me! By the time I reached age thirty and was thoroughly addicted to the nicotine habit, I discovered that all the same problems were with me. I didn't have to "discover" them. They had been pushed into a little corner of my computer filed under "A" for "Avoid"—they finally just popped back to reality. At thirty I had to go back to age sixteen when I'd stopped solving my problems as they came along and had to start all over. Only I wasn't sixteen, and I had three children and a husband to take care of. I had to start tackling those problems of insecurity, defiance, and rebellion without "friend" cigarette.

Sometimes I still wake up in the mornings filled with awe that I actually kicked that habit. It's really exciting to face the day knowing that an addictive drug is no longer going to make decisions for me. Some mornings I wake up after having the best "smoking dreams." I go to sleep, my computer flips onto "subconscious" and I get to smoke for the night. When I wake up I feel great because I got to experience smoking without actually smoking, and I don't have to feel guilty. This leads to the question, "Well, does that mean that after you quit smoking you'll want them and crave them for the rest of your life?" Of course not—but cigarettes are "passing thoughts" like a lot of other thoughts. I don't feel frantic for want of one. They are part of my past because they were part of me. Anything we experience becomes a part of us. What is important is that when it is time to let an experience go, you let it go and take up a new experience.

Do I sound dramatic? You bet! Becoming addicted to nicotine is a dramatic experience and when you withdraw it is a dramatic experience. Each year you smoke, it may become more difficult to quit because cigarettes become more and more a part of your being and your problem-solving mechanism. I curse that first cigarette. I curse the "powers that be" for not letting us know that we were dealing with one of the most powerful addictions there is. Most of all, I curse myself for getting so wrapped up in them that it was almost impossible to live without them.

1. **HOW FORTUNATE THIS GENERATION IS TO KNOW THE TRUTH.** How fortunate this generation is to have mental health facilities, group rap sessions, and school counselors to talk to about the feelings you are having where growing up and accepting adult responsibilities are concerned.

As young people it is so easy to think, "Oh well, what do I care what happens at age thirty or age forty—that is really over-the-hill and gone." But I have one guarantee for you. You'll not only still care, but it will be the most exciting time of your life if you will let it be so. Do you think that Sally Fields, Cheryl Tiegs, Jane Fonda, Mary Tyler Moore, Clint Eastwood, Paul Newman, Robert Redford, Dustin Hoffman, and many other celebrities have gone over the hill and are lying in life's rut? None of them would go back to being age twenty again! There's no doubt—you've got the tough times.

If you blow it now, you will end up one of those "over-thirty/over-the-hill" types. There are plenty of human beings like that who refused to "get up and fight." They refused to find life a challenge. They resented the fact that life isn't always fair. So they learned to depend on pills, booze, overwork, cigarettes, and anything else that dulled their pain. Now they are "over the hill." But they made that choice themselves. So can you. So what if you fall while you're trying to get to the "top of the hill"? When you were a little kid and you fell, you got back up and kept going. What has happened in the meantime? What makes us all become human chickens? What makes us quit thinking for ourselves so that we become human sheep? Whoever told us that we were born with a guarantee that "life is easy"? The only people on this earth who have life easy are your fellow beings over in the cemetery. And I bet they'd all have given us smoking if it meant being alive like you.

So, what I'm trying to help you understand is that you need to quit NOW. Quit while you can. Remember that you'll still care when you are thirty, forty, or whatever age. The joy and pain you feel today will still be there, but it will be stronger, and you'll have the "gift of years" to help you deal with it.

2. **YOUR PARENTS HAVE THE SAME FEELINGS YOU HAVE.** Some have learned to share them with you. Some have learned to deal with them. Some just try to escape by covering them up with drinking, smoking, overworking, etc. Don't judge them harshly. Just do better than they, and only then will you be able to help them. They're doing their best with what they have been given and taught. Just do your best. They are afraid just like you are. For those who have smoking parents, consider them as equal human beings with equal feelings, and ask them why they can't stop smoking. Some of their answers may be just what you need to quit now—for good. Some have been cursing their habit for years. Some have warned you not ever to take it up. Some will pretend they like their smoking habit. As long as someone has a habit, they need to defend

it. Just like I pretended I liked my smoking habit. I <u>had</u> to pretend. My ego was too big to admit that cigarettes <u>controlled</u> my whole life. I don't like being wrong. Most smokers don't like to be wrong. But I'm learning to be wrong and am becoming stronger <u>learning</u> from my mistakes than denying they exist.

3. **PLEASE <u>DON'T</u> CONTINUALLY NAG AT YOUR PARENTS IF THEY SMOKE.** Tell them how you feel but don't become the "smoking judge." When my daughters nagged me, the little child in me came out and, instead of quitting, I'd go into the bathroom and step up on the toilet so I could secretly blow the smoke out the bathroom window, like a fat person runs to the refrigerator for comfort when someone nags at their eating habit. A silly game to play, but I didn't like being caught "being wrong."

4. **ASK YOUR PARENTS HOW IT REALLY IS TO BE A LIFETIME SMOKER.** They might give you answers that will convince you nicotine is one of the most addictive drugs known to man and one you don't need to tangle with. If they <u>can't</u> give you an answer, you might get the answer even more clearly.

The fact remains that even if you hate smoking, if you watch your parents turn to their cigarettes in stress situations over a long period of time, you may start to copy them. We tend to learn from our parents, whether we are learning negative or positive habits. Just remember you have a choice to smoke or not to smoke. Just close your eyes and talk to yourself about it like we all did when we were little kids, and no one thought we were weird then. It was normal for little kids to go down the street talking to themselves. Ask yourself what you really want to do. You'll give yourself the right answer . . . then stick with it.

Some of you have parents who seem to be very successful in their lives even though they smoke. The fact remains that all their success will do them little good after they have destroyed their bodies. If they were <u>really</u> in command of their own lives, they wouldn't need to "keep puffing" to keep up with the rest of us.

You also may have heard, "If your parents love you, they wouldn't smoke." Baloney! Of course they love you. It just shows that for <u>some</u> people, nicotine is a stronger compeller than love. And that is strong! Get the message? Why would you want to deal with an opponent <u>stronger</u> than love?

Others may point out that intelligent people don't smoke. Not true. Some of the most intelligent people are addicted to cigarettes, booze, pills. "SMARTS" have nothing to do with addictions . . . but AWARENESS does. They just become temporarily ignorant when their addictions take over. <u>The intelligent ones who pass the final exam are the ones who get help for their addiction.</u> It also takes intelligence of sorts to think up the rationales for smoking. Of course they only sound intelligent to other smokers. To those who don't smoke, they sound pathetic.

The point to be made is that you may <u>start</u> smoking for reasons such as peer pressure, weight control, problem-solving, relaxation, but you'll <u>continue</u> to smoke because you are addicted to nicotine. You'll no longer be in command of your life. You will spend more time with your cigarettes than you do with anyone else. You WON'T be able to go more than a few hours without them. You WON'T be able to make major decisions without them. You may think you look beautiful or masculine smoking cigarettes. But what is beautiful or manly about burning holes in your clothes, cars, and furniture? What is beautiful or sensuous about smelling like a dirty ashtray? What is sensuous about bad breath? What is beautiful about being "emphysema thin?" What is masculine about burning a hole in your child someday because you can't put your cigarette down long enough to love him or her? And what is great about spending 400 to 600 bucks a year to kill yourself?

5. **ALL OF US HAVE BEEN TAKEN IN BY THE TOBACCO INDUSTRY.** It strikes at young people where it really hurts—it takes advantages of the _pain_ of being young. It really tries to convince you that you'll be VIRGINIA SLIM, KOOL, have VANTAGE, have MORE, be TRIUMPHant, and smooth as the lump on a CAMEL's back. In reality, you won't be any of these. You'll just be paying lots of money to get yourself _addicted_. The tobacco industry counts on your trying to smoke just for fun and pleasure, but within a year you'll be a steady customer. You'll end up "paying money to treat yourself badly!"

Don't let cigarettes become such a part of you that you can't part with them. Remain the master of your own mind and body. Sometimes it's a lonely road, but it's a guarantee to "staying on top of the hill." The people piled at the bottom of the hill let someone else control their minds and bodies.

If you don't smoke yet, please don't start. If you are already smoking, quit now. If you need help to quit, get help. Go through the few miserable days of nicotine withdrawal now—it will be many times worse later on. The more you smoke, the more cigarettes control you. Don't worry about gaining weight; just exercise more and eat less. If you're still hungry and feeling sorry for yourself, cut a straw in half and puff on it. For some reason it really makes you feel better. If someone asks what you're doing, just tell them, "I'M SMOKING A STRAW." Stock up on sugarless gum and mints. Carry a miniature box of raisins.

You are still young and have abundant energy to conquer the cigarette habit. You may feel afraid and lonely without them for awhile. They have been a sort of friend to you, and we always feel lonely when a friend has gone. Well, tell them to get lost; you'll start to feel better. If your friends give you a bad time about not smoking with them anymore, just tell them you won't bug them about _their_ smoking, if they don't bug you about _not_ smoking. Fair? Besides, your friends won't always be around, but you will. So account only to yourself. BE YOUR OWN BEST FRIEND.

XI

How Family, Friends, and Co-Workers Can Help

"It takes strength to ask for help—and the strong are willing to give it."—L.B.

This is probably <u>the most important chapter of all</u>. Breaking <u>any</u> addiction is very difficult without a support system. If you are a smoker who is trying to quit smoking, copy these few pages and pass them around to those near to you, and to those who are working with you.

IF YOU ARE A NON-SMOKER buying this book for a "smoking friend," be sure that this is the chapter you read. Buying the book for them is only the first step. The most important step is being a friend who supports them while they are quitting. Here are a few rules to the game of being a true supporter:

1. **NO NAGGING.** Nagging does <u>not</u> make a person stop smoking. Only the person smoking can do that. Doctors are the exception; they can exert a very positive and demanding influence on the smoker.

   Nagging only makes a person feel more guilty for having disappointed you. <u>When they feel guilty, they feel degraded and angry.</u> And <u>when they feel this way, their only "true friend and supporter" is their cigarette.</u> So, they'll have one to deal with their feelings of frustration or inadequacy. Not nagging is easier said than done: I can become a champion nagger when I think the need arises. But we have to keep working on not using nagging as a tool against the smoker.

   <u>Only encouragement, a good listener's ear, and positive words are allowed.</u> If you really want them to quit, it has to be that way. Stop and think how you felt when someone in your life nagged and belittled you for something they felt you shouldn't do. Did it make you feel energetic and positive about tackling the problem? Or did it make you feel defeated and hurt? Let's say that it was overeating—bet you ran to the refrigerator instead. At least the refrigerator didn't nag at you. It gave you temporary comfort. A smoker will run to the pack of cigarettes when nagged. Cigarettes and refrigerators and whiskey bottles—true friends? No, but they seem to be when "righteous" people enter the scene. "So, when you feel the urge to nag, stuff your mouth with a rag."

2. **NO SELF-RIGHTEOUSNESS.** Lead yourself down your <u>own</u> path of righteousness, but don't worry about the path of righteousness for the smoker's sake. They already feel lowly for smoking. If you gave up cigarettes very easily, they really don't want to hear about your "tower of will power." <u>Your</u> accomplishment was only <u>your</u> way of dealing with your problems. Each smoker deals with the smoking problem in a different way. It has nothing to do with your

81

being stronger than they are. Please do not have "self-righteous attacks." Besides, the universe deals harshly with the self-righteous. I know. The times I've had "self-righteous attacks" the little "humbling man" follows right behind me and gets me every time. It's called "being given the opportunity to learn."

It's different if you have something to share about your smoking experience that will make their situation more comfortable. Then you're on the same side rather than on opposite sides. And traditionally the cheering crowd is on the same side as those they are rooting for. Sharing your own pain in accomplishing a goal may actually help you to relive the experience. Then you'll remember how difficult it was, rather than how easy it was now that it is past history. This leads to compassion and empathy. I have said this before and I'll say it again, "Why would anyone want to give up a smoking habit if all the ex-smokers in the world are self-righteous and miserable? Set an example—if you are really comfortable with having given up whatever habit you have given up, you will be compassionate and supportive. If you are still miserable and deprived after having given up your habit, you really didn't understand your habit enough to let it go. It's still morbidly written all over your face and showing in your attitude.

I am far from perfect about never feeling self-righteous. People whom I love and care about very much still smoke, and I'm put to the test daily. Sometimes I don't pass the test, but I'm learning. I can sense a "self-righteous attack" coming on. What I try to do is figure out what is really wrong in my life. As I get my life back on track, it's very interesting to find I'm not as worried about other people being perfect. I work on my own perfection. That should keep me busy for a lifetime.

So, when you feel a "righteous attack" coming, either leave the scene or shut your mouth. Or go discuss it with a neutral person to get it out of your system. Or put your face into a pillow and shout. What this all amounts to is that if you can't be supportive, you can't be effective. When we get attacks of self-righteousness, it would be wiser to spend our time figuring out why we have appointed ourselves earthly judges over our fellow human beings.

3. **GIVE LOTS OF LOVE, HUGGING AND TENDER CARE.** This rule will help you be the best support system available. When smokers are quitting and seem very short-tempered, don't take it personally. They aren't really angry with you. They are angry at themselves for having gotten into this addiction mess in the first place, and they'll take it out on the first person who shows their face. Be mature enough to not take it personally.

During the first few days of nicotine withdrawal, the body chemistry is really confused. This makes the smokers appear confused. They often feel frantic. Or lightheaded. Or sleepy. Or angry. Or hyperactive. They lash our because of this state of confusion. They feel lonely without their cigarettes, and foolish because of them. Take time to ask if they want to share their feelings. If they don't tell them you are available whenever they do feel like sharing. But listen only. Or you can help them with menial or boring tasks. If they love back rubs, give them many. Help them feel less pressure by taking them out to dinner. Or by cooking dinner. Or by doing up the dishes or mowing the lawn. Sending flowers can do magic. A card or a special gift can make the difference between a bad day or a good day.

AFTER THE FIRST FEW DAYS, the intensity of their frantic feelings will diminish. The mood changes will be spaced farther apart. The most important, and most difficult, thing to do is not to take the verbal lashings seriously at the moment. If real issues arise, save them for more tranquil times. This may be the only way they're able to express themselves now. With time and support, smokers will learn to deal with their feelings on a new, realistic level. The feelings are flowing out though. The "cigarette plug" has been pulled and choice words may flow. Many marriages, relationships, and working situations have actually become better because an ex-smoker has stopped playing polite word games, and the truth is out in the open. It may hurt for awhile, but if all concerned are willing to deal with the truth, a deeper and more sincere relationship can emerge. Once the new feelings are out, don't be afraid of them or pretend they don't exist. Deal with them when all people involved have clamed down. If it is too difficult to do alone, get professional help. It takes strength to ask for help. Only the strong do. Keep loving them, and it will come back to you many times over.

1. **SMOKING IS A HABIT THAT TAKES A VERY LONG TIME TO LEARN.** It cannot be unlearned in a day's time. If you refuse to give them time to unlearn the smoking habit, they may just replace it with another negative habit such as overeating, drinking, or becoming plain mean. During this challenging time, it will take your love, acceptance, patience, and support. Have you got them?

2. **THE FIRST FEW WEEKS ARE THE HARDEST FOR THE EX-SMOKER.** Although some people seem to breeze through the first few days, eventually they'll have some hard times. These are harder to accept because they thought it wouldn't happen. Again, this is just the individuality of each smoker emerging. Some contain their pain inside, and when it finally comes splashing out like an unleashed dam, it can drown those around them in surprise and confusion. Keep cool, and accept this belated overflow. It will not last forever.

3. **THEY MAY SEEM EXTREMELY SENSITIVE TO ANYTHING THAT IS SAID.** You ask them to take the garbage out and they may snap at you. You ask them to bring you some coffee and they may tell you off. Please be patient and remember this sort of attitude improves with each day and each week. All concerned need to really take it a day at a time. When they have bad days after a period of tranquility, don't be afraid they're going to start smoking again. They are just having a bad day like you and I are entitled to have every so often. Bad days are dealt out to smokers and ex-smokers.

You can be of great help by seeing that there are always plenty of cigarette substitutes handy. Plastic straws are great for hand and mouth distraction. Puffing on them can actually be relaxing. Oxygen is taken in at about the same pace as when smoking; this can be comforting. Toothpicks may be preferred instead. Cinnamon-flavored ones would be a treat if you can find them. Keep sugarless gum, mints, or lemon drops handy for them at home, in the office, or the car, etc. Sunflower seeds (with shells) keep the ex-smoker's hands and mouth very busy. Lollipops take a long time to devour and come in handy the first few weeks. Check with their doctor if they can't have sweets. Ice water by their chair is comforting for some ex-smokers. If they feel ANGRY, give them cigarette advertisements to cut into little pieces.

4. **SOME OF US WHO QUITE SMOKING COMPARE IT TO LOSING A BEST FRIEND.** A best friend is usually someone who has been around for a long time, accepts us as we are, loves us, is always there when we need them, and doesn't nag at us. Cigarettes fit all of these qualifications. When we lose a friend, we feel lonely and empty and scattered inside. This is how smokers feel when they have to give up their cigarettes. You may think this is crazy, but this is how people feel giving up any addiction. Perhaps you have only seen cigarettes as the big, deadly enemy to health and self-respect. You can't imagine them as having been friends unless you have smoked.

And for some of you, they never became friends. You didn't let them, and gave them up before they became that close to you. But you're not the friend or mate who is going through withdrawal now, so be patient if they tend to mourn this loss. What <u>really</u> matters is that the smoker has chosen to <u>end</u> this friendship with smoking. Accept this loss as painful to them. Whenever separation or death occurs in a relationship of any kind, the next stage is to mourn. Only after mourning can you accept the finality. <u>So let them mourn</u>. If they are allowed to mourn, they can get on with the act of being a non-smoker. They will still have memories of the smoking habit, but memories are badges of survival.

When the person you are trying to help happens to SNEAK a cigarette in the stop-smoking process, PLEASE DON'T SAY, "I <u>told</u> you you couldn't do it." It hasn't helped in the past . . . has it? No guilt or guilt-showering is allowed in the stop-smoking process. <u>Guilt only leads to self-depreciation, which leads to self-punishment, which leads to going back to smoking.</u> We need to think of this project as a very long race—many miles . . . many hours . . . many weeks. If the person stumbles in the race (has a cigarette), we need to encourage them to get back on their feet and into the race (and thinking like an ex-smoker again). If they fall flat on their face in a puddle (have many cigarettes), they already have a big enough price to pay . . . don't rub the mud in. They'll have to start the race all over again (go through withdrawal again) . . . so if they lose a <u>few</u> miles in the race, keep cheering them on. This is not a race of who gets there <u>first</u>. All that counts is that they finally get to the finish line. Some are fast, some are slow, and some just like the sound of the starting gun. The race can be won with enough supporters on the sidelines. How would <u>you</u> feel if it were <u>your</u> race and everyone was laughing, booing, and blocking the way? Be a supporter.

<u>You have the ability, the intelligence, and the power to help this person become an ex-smoker.</u> They must do it themselves, but having a support system feels good. You are close to this person. You care about this person if you took the time to read this chapter. And they care about what <u>you</u> think of them. Can you help them feel positive about their stop-smoking process? And about themselves? They are strong to be quitting cigarettes, and you are strong to be supporting them. THANK YOU FOR HELPING THEM TO BECOME SUCCESSFUL EX-SMOKERS.

To My Intimate Support System

I just made a big decision, a decision that is frightening as well as challenging. I have chosen to quit smoking!!

I have also chosen to feel the joy and the pain of this task. I cannot pretend to be "Macho Man/Woman" and just throw my cigarettes over my shoulder riding off into the non-smoking sunset.

I smoked for many years. I might even have smoked cigarettes more times than I ate, slept, or kissed you goodbye. Cigarettes were my friend and comfort, as well as my addiction and my humbling.

I feel vulnerable and I know it is O.K. to feel that way. I can't experience personal growth without feeling vulnerable. I cannot take risks without feeling vulnerable. PLEASE . . . do not violate my vulnerability.

I chose you because I feel safe with you. Please do not violate that safety and love by making sarcastic comments, by criticizing my program, by rejecting my feelings, by acting ashamed of my tears, by rejecting my anger.

I need you now. I need your support. I respect the pain you are feeling because I seem to be changing all the "ground rules" of our relationship. I need you to share your pain and fear with me.

I cherish our relationship enough to make it better. I am willing to become real, vulnerable and genuine. I may express too much anger, sadness and joy for awhile. My cigarette plugged many of these emotions for many years. Help me to welcome these new emotions.

Learn to "fight fair" with me by sharing how you feel. Learn to fight for your right to express your feelings . . . even if I don't appreciate them right away. I will in time.

Let's fight for us . . . we are worth saving! You are not my enemy. I am not your enemy. We once chose each other. Let's close our eyes together and remember how we once felt about each other. Then let us open our eyes and see each other with "new" eyes . . . with "soft" eyes.

Support me through this transition and I will support you through your next transition . . . we are worth it!

Linda R. Bryson
© 1985

"If NAGGING really worked, NAGGING CLINICS would be springing up all over the nation. If NAGGING really worked, someone would be making a profit off the technique!"—Linda R. Bryson

What a Smoking Friend Can Do to Help

1. There are so many things that friends enjoy doing together such as eating, drinking, and, best of all, SMOKING.

2. Your friend or family member has made a decision to quit smoking. It is one of the biggest decisions they will ever make. THEY NEED YOUR HELP MOST OF ALL. It is bad enough having been nagged by society to quit. When they finally take the big step, they don't need friends encouraging them back to smoking; they need your positive support.

3. Their physical, emotional, and spiritual health may be at stake if they continue to smoke. Please do all you can to set them up for SUCCESS.

4. The first few weeks after a smoker quits smoking finds them so vulnerable to having "just one cigarette" for old time's sake. Smoking has been a form of companionship, and they may feel a little guilty for not being able to smoke with you. WOULD YOU PLEASE HELP THEM FIND ANOTHER FORM OF COMPANIONSHIP THAT YOU CAN STILL ENJOY TOGETHER?

5. During the first few days of nicotine withdrawal, another smoker's smoke can smell DELICIOUS . . . this is all it takes to tempt the ex-smoker back to smoking. It won't kill you to step outside to smoke, but it might kill them if they go back to smoking when their health is at stake. PLEASE DON'T SMOKE IN THEIR HOME OR CAR UNTIL THEY ARE SECURE WITHOUT THEIR CIGARETTES. SHOW THEM THIS THOUGHTFULNESS AND THEY WON'T BUG YOU ABOUT YOUR SMOKING.

6. If you are traveling in a car together, you can plan to take "smoking stops" along the way. The smell of a cigarette in a small enclosed area like a car can be too tempting. PLEASE REMEMBER THAT ALL IT TAKES FOR US EX-SMOKERS TO GET STARTED ALL OVER AGAIN IS "ONE LITTLE PUFF."

7. If the smoker is having "grumpy days," please refrain from comments like, "Why don't you go back to smoking and be your nice old self again?" They might take you up on it because your friendship means a lot to them. However, you're fighting dirty; you might need to ask yourself why you resent their success at kicking the cigarette habit. After all, they've pulled "the cigarette plug," and they may talk more and express their feelings more easily. IF YOU ARE A TRUE FRIEND, YOU WILL ALLOW THEM THESE IMPERFECTIONS AS THEY ALLOW YOURS.

8. Change is frightening to all of us, whether it is negative or positive. It is easier to stay in a comfortable rut where we feel safe. Actually, we aren't safe; we are only rusting away. Change can be challenging; it doesn't have to be frightening. It all depends on your attitude. They have had to change their attitude to quit smoking. PLEASE ALLOW THEM THIS CHANGE. HELP THEM FEEL SECURE DURING THIS CHANGE!!

9. Make a pact with your friend. You make it easier for them to quit smoking and they will promise never to become a self-righteous ex-smoker.

10. And what is the best of all—if and when you decide to quit smoking, your act of friendship and support during their crisis will always be remembered and appreciated. THEY WILL BE A SUPPORTIVE FRIEND TO YOU IF YOU DECIDE TO QUIT.

XII
The Real Price That Women Pay for Smoking

"Women are fighting for freedom—why create another 'trap'?"—
L. B.

Much information is available to the public on the negative impact the pregnant mother who smokes has on the fetus or the nursing mother who smokes has on her newborn child. Their babies tend to be smaller, more premature, and have a higher neonatal death rate. I want to emphasize this because THESE TINY, INNOCENT BABIES HAVE NO CHOICE. If their own mothers won't defend them, I will. I was guilty of smoking during one of my three pregnancies, but I was ignorant of the facts. In 1960, the first studies were conducted that showed the damage done to fetuses and newborns of smoking mothers. Now we all know better. No doctor alive would recommend that a pregnant or nursing mother smoke cigarettes.

The mother has a choice whether or not to smoke. The fetus or newborn does not have this choice. Babies receive carbon monoxide through placental transfer of the pregnant mother and through the milk of the nursing mother. They can be damaged without their consent.

SMOKING IS MUCH MORE CRUEL TO WOMEN THAN IT IS TO MEN. Think of the premature wrinkling and aging effect on women who smoke. There is a decrease of approximately 15 to 20 percent in circulation of the facial capillaries. The already minute capillaries are constricted even more by smoking, which cuts down on the supply of blood and nutrients to the skin. With decreased circulation, women cease to glow. They take on a sallow, pasty, yellowed look after smoking for a few years. Good circulation is the key to beauty—all the makeup in the world cannot cover an undernourished skin. OUTWARD BEAUTY COMES FROM INWARD NOURISHMENT.

When MEN get premature wrinkles, people say, "Isn't he aging nicely?" When WOMEN lose their skin tone and get premature wrinkles from smoking, no one says they are aging nicely. Facial comments are avoided; compliments are made on body features, but your body is not the key to your character. Your face is the key to your character; why ruin it? Doesn't life already deal out enough "character lines" in return for our laughter, our tears, and our survival? I decided that smoking was not going to add to them unnecessarily. With their new freedom, women can also be free to make choices that slow down the aging process—or they can hasten it! HEALTHY AGING IS BEAUTIFUL—CHOOSE AND CHERISH IT!

When a woman smokes cigarettes, she spends approximately one-third of the day with her mouth puckered into a sucking position. It's no wonder that after ten or more years of smoking, the creases around the mouth from the sucking position become permanent pictures. What we're doing when we smoke is putting an invisible brace on the mouth area that will eventually accomplish its purpose. Also there is the invisible bracing of crows' feet around the eyes from the continual squinting the face does in order to protect itself from the onslaught of smoke to the eyes.

Smoking women very seldom have clear, bright eyes. What is so very rewarding to me when women stop smoking is the reward they have when they look in the mirror two or three weeks later. They like the relaxed, serene look that their face is beginning to have again. Looking in the mirror becomes fun again—whether it's from seeing a fresh look, or a new, fresh attitude about themselves.

There will always be the exception to the wrinkling rule. A few women with extraordinary heredity may prove me wrong. But there are only a few women out of millions. They may not get the wrinkling, but they'll still get the toughened, leathery look.

Please remember that I am not putting down the aging process. This can be a very rewarding and positive process and cannot be avoided. I'm only putting down a negative and deliberate attempt to hasten the process. Doctors seem to disagree about whether the wrinkling can be reversed after a woman stops smoking. In women who are still fairly young, or those fortunate women with good elasticity and circulation in the facial area, there is hope. I believe this to be true because I have witnessed people during severely stressful times in their acquire a very wrinkled, haggard look. When their lives become tranquil again, the aging process seemed to reverse itself, and they took on a refreshed look with the wrinkles seeming to have ironed themselves out. Medically feasible or not, I believe in the power of physical healing through the art of positive thinking and change. If you believe you look better, you will feel better, and henceforth you will look better.

Observant doctors state that they can immediately determine if a female patient is a smoker by the yellowed nostrils, teeth, and fingers of longtime smokers. The gums of smokers will not be in as healthy a condition as non-smokers, and, of course, the smell of cigarettes in the hair and clothing is an immediate giveaway.

Again, you'll always be looking for the exceptions if you are looking for excuses to continue smoking. There will be those women who do not suffer the effects until their 70's and 80's. The reason you hear about them is because they are exceptions; the press seldom raves about people who take care of themselves. Only the person who drinks, smokes, and overeats gets press coverage when they live to be 100 years of age. After all, the average person who treasures his health, believes in the quality of life, and refuses to smoke can be very boring. The fact is that if any of us wants and believes in the quality of life, we have to take care of ourselves. Most of us have only average heredity to fall back onto, and have unhealthy environmental factors and everyday stresses that demand we take care of ourselves. If you've been given the unusual gift of strong heredity, why would you want to flaunt it in the faces of those who must take care of themselves to receive the quality of life? Anyone can have a long life. Some of us just choose not to be hooked on pills, or to carry an oxygen tank around because we have emphysema from smoking.

Do I sound condescending to my fellow sisters for making them seem ignorant for smoking? I don't mean to. The only condescending bunch is the tobacco industry which makes women appear sensuous, popular, confident, and intelligent for making the choice to smoke. In reality, women who smoke cannot be sensuous when they smell like stale cigarette smoke. I really didn't believe that I stank when I was a smoker. I believed it was a plot of the non-smokers to harass me. When my daughter quit smoking she asked me, "Mom, did I really smell like that lady who smokes?"

And as far as being popular, you can only be popular with the smoking crowd. Non-smokers, children and little animals will try to avoid you when at all possible. Do you really become more confident when you smoke as suggested by cigarette advertising? You may appear more confident because you are not expressing your true feelings and can play the "Miss Cool Act." All you're doing is plugging your mouth with the cigarette plug. Why not pull it and get to know yourself?

Regarding intelligent women smoking: yes, intelligent women smoke, but in their hearts they <u>know</u> their lives are controlled by nicotine and they cannot make a decision without nicotine. It's a degrading feeling. No matter how well-dressed and coiffured a woman may be, she blows the whole cool act when she lights up—she loses her independence. Her <u>dependence</u> shows. I considered myself a very intelligent smoker, but when other people confronted me with these harsh realities, the rationales for continuing to smoke seemed senseless.

THE TOBACCO INDUSTRY IS NOT YOUR FRIEND. It only wants women to continue believing its ads and buying its cigarettes. Smokers who get lung cancer and <u>sue</u> the tobacco companies <u>never</u> win. The tobacco industry counteracts with the statement, "You read the dangers on the label." It is protected legally and may continue to kill you—legally. As a volunteer driving lung cancer and throat cancer patients to radiation therapy, I wonder if anyone has ever asked the tobacco industry to send out volunteers to drive these people back and forth for treatment. But don't bother calling—you'll be put on Hold, <u>forever</u>.

The young woman reading this book may think, "Oh well, by the time I get to be thirty or forty years of age, I'll be over the hill and won't care anyway how I look." <u>But women of today know that our best and most exciting years are over age thirty</u>, and most of us feel more beautiful and useful than we ever felt at age twenty. Do you think women like Sophia Loren, Cheryl Tiegs, Jane Fonda, and other plus-30's feel "over the hill"? They're at the "top of the hill," and they all take care of themselves. Cheryl Tiegs, as well as many other models who advertised cigarettes, would not smoke themselves. <u>Models would not look good in closeups if they smoked</u>. But in the meantime, too many young women are imitating the models by taking up a habit that most models wouldn't even consider. Advertisers forget to mention that the models do not use the product.

It's also a MAN'S WORLD when it comes to developing the "smoker's voice." This is the gravelly, monotonic voice that women who have smoked for a long period of time get. When Dean Martin, or some other male's, voice gets lower and lower the more years they have smoked, we hear: "How sensuous and low his voice is getting." <u>But does anyone compliment the woman who starts to sound like "Gravel Gertie"?</u> Not really—even Lauren Bacall has stopped smoking—her voice was naturally low and sensuous; the next stage would have been raspy, monotonous, and man-like. She also saw her husband, Humphrey Bogart, die from lung cancer. I have noticed many female singers who smoke and can no longer <u>project</u> their voices—and amplification cannot cover up inadequacy and lack of tone and quality.

So many of us continued to smoke because we were afraid of getting fat. In the past this was a problem. But it was only a problem because it was not discussed, just taken for granted. Read the chapter on weight control and you'll see that it does not need to be a problem. It will only become one if you keep saying that you will get fat. Then you will!!

What we do is destroy the inside of our bodies, eventually messing up the outside, and all because we think we can't be thin unless we smoke. <u>What has happened to our sense of values?</u> <u>As long as we look thin from a distance, who cares if we look unhealthy up close?</u> Whom are we trying to impress? STRANGERS—people we don't even know? What about those CLOSE to us—who must smell us and watch us destroy ourselves internally and externally? <u>For the chance to look thin, we'll trade in our self-respect, our self-control, our health, our fresh glow in the facial area, and our lives!</u> I've talked to so many husbands and boyfriends who are grateful to have a fresh-smelling woman again. Nicotine, with perfume to cover it up, just plain stinks!

CIGARETTE ADS MAY SHOW SENSUOUS WOMEN, but they <u>won't</u> tell you about the increase in lung cancer in women that now equals that in males. Is that sensuous? What's sensuous about a woman dying at age forty from lung cancer? Or losing all her hair from chemotherapy? <u>She has finally fulfilled her dream to be thin; she's only eighty pounds the week before she dies and she wishes she weren't thin anymore.</u> What is sensuous about trying to explain to your children and grandchildren that you're sorry you won't live to see them grow up? And all because you believed that some tobacco leaves in a wrap-around white cover would "light up your life"!

The surgeon general has reported that by 1983 more women will be dying from smoking-related diseases—such as cancer and heart disease—than from breast cancer. Everyone knows someone with breast cancer or who has survived breast cancer. Can you imagine meeting <u>more</u> women with lung cancer? You <u>WON'T—because only five percent of them will survive a five-year period. For every woman you meet who survives, you won't meet the nineteen who DIDN'T.</u> This is <u>liberation</u>?

The Tobacco Institute had no comment on this finding. Why? Because they finally got caught with their hands in the money jar. Women have been ripped off into believing they had free choice. How do you really have free choice when you are dealing with an addictive drug? Women didn't start smoking in such large numbers as men until twenty to thirty years ago. This is just about the time needed to grow a cancerous tumor.

So now is when the "true harvest" of the tobacco industry will be reaped, and it is <u>the only winner</u> in this sick cash market. If you get lung cancer, don't complain to <u>them</u>—they'll tell you you had a "free choice."

The only way you can fight back is to never buy another cigarette, and to convince those around you to follow suit. Quit buying magazines that sponsor cigarette advertising, and write and tell publishers WHY. Start looking at each cigarette advertisement; <u>analyze it</u> to see what psychological impression they are trying to make.

DO I CARE? If I didn't, I'd be lecturing for the <u>Tobacco Institute</u> and saying KIND words to you instead of the TRUTH!

"Cigarettes have been the 'punctuation marks' of my life—the PAUSES, the PERIODS, the QUESTION MARKS, and the EXCLAMATION POINTS!"—Merrie Ziady

"When I quit smoking, I let another one of my black clouds go."

XIII
How to Stay Off Cigarettes Forever

"Understanding the power of your habit will eliminate that power."—L. B.

After you've been through the withdrawal from nicotine, you may think that the stop-smoking game is all over and you've won. But when you are able to accept that the game is just beginning, then success is guaranteed. If you don't build strong lines of defense against the trigger mechanisms that activate your desire for cigarettes, you may have to go back to the bench and warm up all over again.

TRIGGER MECHANISMS are the little comfortable smoking reminders stored in your computer that are activated when the smoking habit confronts you. For instance, you want to get together with an old friend you haven't seen for awhile. You meet, sit down for lunch, and the friend lights up. Your personal computer says, "Friend is smoking; please send out program that calls for me to smoke with friend—pleasant sensations will follow." Your need has been activated. This can happen months, even years from now. Don't be afraid—just accept how your mind works and be prepared. What will you do? Go call a buddy to distract yourself? Pull a straw out and start puffing? Or be honest and tell the friend you're having a nicotine fit that will be over within three minutes, and you don't want to give in to it?

This is not negative thinking—this is reality. Be prepared for reality, and then tackle it in a positive manner. The first couple of years that I worked with smokers in groups and on a personal basis, there were always a certain number who made it. Some made it with ease; others made it with agony. But when I called those successful ex-smokers three to six months later to see how they were doing, half of them were back on cigarettes. Why? The timing wasn't right for a few, and they have since made it successfully. Others just refused to accept the reality that, "It is easier to quit than it is to stay off." It can be compared to planting a garden. Some people actually think that all you do is plant the seeds and plants magically grow while weeds magically disappear. It is easy to plant seeds, but difficult to maintain a garden. This is not a negative statement, just reality. Successful people of all cultures live by this code.

I asked the smokers who had gone back to smoking how they felt about it. The reactions were self-disgust and disappointment in themselves. But they were too aware to say they'll never try again. Most of them will make it when they can accept the concepts of taking one day at a time when quitting smoking and remembering that tomorrow will bring the success they've been waiting for.

What so many smoking programs have done in the past, and I did also, was to teach people how to QUIT, but not how to STAY OFF. So people reacted to the trigger mechanisms that activated the desire to smoke during old comfortable, or uncomfortable, situations. They had agreed with nicotine's forces that started "talking" in their heads about, "Oh go ahead and have just one little cigarette. You're an adult capable of making intelligent decisions." Like the alcoholic who

91

Post this HALT! process on your refrigerator or desk—sometimes we have a cigarette only because we are really hungry, angry, lonely or tired—please be aware that self-awareness increases success!

H. HUNGRY.	**A.** ANGRY.	**L.** LONELY.	**T. !** TIRED.
AM I HUNGRY? Do I feel "something is missing?" When we get that feeling of emptiness, we often are not able to decide whether we want food or a cigarette—all we know is that we want "something".	AM I ANGRY? Do I feel that my anger is a valid excuse to have a cigarette?	AM I LONELY? Feeling lonely can be overwhelming enough to send us back to smoking. Again, we need to tell ourselves that feeling lonely is alright, but what we do with that lonely feeling may not be alright for us and for others.	AM I TIRED? All of us feel more vulnerable when we are tired. We begin the relapse process which deludes us into thinking that the only way we can be re-energized is to "stoke our fires with a cigarette."
Smokers can miss a meal because they often don't want to take the time to eat—instead they just "eat smoke."	Please remember that we can still be worthwhile people when we are feeling angry—we don't have to punish ourselves with a cigarette. We don't need to "stuff" down those angry feelings with a cigarette!	When I am feeling lonely, I need to take self-responsibility and admit that I created my lonely feelings.	If this was the way our bodies were meant to be energized, we would have all been born with cigarettes in our mouth!
If you have become a non-smoker, you can't afford to miss a meal—it is guaranteed to leave you feeling "hungry". Although your body is calling for food, your addiction is calling for nicotine.	ANGER IS A VALID EMOTION. ANGER IS NOT A VALID EXCUSE FOR HAVING A CIGARETTE.	Being alone does not need to be as lonely if we can appreciate the person we are with—we need to like ourselves and realize we are worthwhile even if we are alone.	If we don't have time to sleep, we can always take a few minutes to do a relaxation technique or a centering technique. People who are truly relaxed or centered have no need for cigarettes!
In the confusion, you may relapse into thinking that only a cigarette will fill in that "empty space."	Feeling angry is alright. What we do with those angry feelings may not be alright for you and others.	Being lonely is a choice. Using loneliness as an excuse to go back to smoking is a choice.	PLEASE GET YOUR REST AND SLEEP. YOU ARE CERTAINLY WORTH IT!
FILL YOUR STOMACH SO THE FEELING OF EMPTINESS DIMINISHES. YOU ARE TOO VULNERABLE TO RELAPSE IF YOU DON'T PRACTICE WELLNESS BY EATING SENSIBLY AND REGULARLY.	Usually when we are angry we need to get in touch with the angry feelings and admit to them—this self-awareness will begin to diminish the angry feelings and reduce the anxiety of the unknown. Ask these questions, "What am I afraid of losing?" "What am I afraid of?"	WE HAVE OTHER CHOICES! Create new hobbies. Become a volunteer. Get counseling or professional help. IT TAKES STRENGTH TO ASK FOR HELP!	
	CALL SOMEONE FOR HELP IF THE ANGER MIGHT LEAD YOU BACK TO SMOKING!		

"takes just one little sip for old time's sake," they are back into the addiction game again. Of course, there are exceptions to this rule. One out of a hundred people can have an occasional puff, but we're only dealing with the ninety-nine out of a hundred who CAN'T! All it takes is the nicotine from ONE cigarette to activate your body chemistry back into the smoking game. Why? Who cares WHY! This is not a technical book; this book is designed to help you stop smoking forever. Technicalities and analytical thinking do not enable us to quit smoking—being honest with ourselves, caring about ourselves, and wanting to be in control of our lives is what enables us to quit.

Let me share some things that some successful ex-smokers have shared with me as to how they reinforced themselves internally not to start smoking again. One ex-smoker says she daily repeats to herself: "I am an ex-smoker." She will do that forever because she knows that smoking can sneak up on you years later; she is making sure that her subconscious knows where she stands! Another ex-smoker has the courage to say: "No thank you, I'm an addict," when she is offered a cigarette at a social gathering. Another ex-smoker asks himself the question: "Do I NEED this cigarette?" He doesn't dare ask himself if he WANTS the cigarette because he might get "yes" for an answer. By asking himself if he NEEDS it, he can honestly say "no." Another ex-smoker still keeps the list of "dislikes" about smoking in plain sight on a cupboard door; when she can't remember WHY she wanted to quit smoking, she can remind herself. Another ex-smoker said whenever he has the desire for a cigarette, he just closes his eyes and remembers how difficult withdrawal was, and he knows if he starts smoking again, even "just a few cigarettes," he'll have to go through withdrawal all over again and he realizes it just isn't worth it! I find that standing in front of the mirror and saying to myself, "I am in control of my life, I am in control of my smoking habit, and I am unwilling to be a smoker" really helps me. You can change the words to fit any goal you hope to achieve—like overeating, drinking, or whatever. It really works if you stick to it long enough.

If you are shaking your head and thinking this all sounds foolish, reread the chapter "On Being a Fool." Foolishness pays off, by your becoming an ex-smoker. If you refuse to make changes in your life, you will have to resign yourself to being a smoker, and will be accepting that NIC-OTINE is to be your master for the rest of your life.

THE KEY TO STAYING OFF CIGARETTES FOREVER COMES BACK TO CONTROL. You want to be in control of your own life, but you cannot be until you have accepted the power of nicotine. Then you are in control because you are accepting reality. Wishful thinking will not keep us from smoking; only positive action and realistic thinking can do this. Alcoholics stay off alcohol because they can admit that alcohol is capable of controlling their lives. They can admit that alcohol has become a part of their total being and controlling it (or letting it control them) is their free choice. It is the same with overeaters. Or compulsive gamblers, drug users, etc.

I do sense an important difference between the needs of alcoholics and cigaretteaholics. Cigaretteaholics often smoke to cover up (or "plug") their feelings; alcoholics often drink to "release" their feelings. What is important is that emotions are not dealt with honestly in either case.

I have received reinforcement to these theories from the ex-smokers I continue to have contact with, some of whom still write me. Being in a small community lends itself to having good follow-up and contact with former and present clients.

I HAVE USED THE SAME TECHNIQUE on myself for other goals I chose to reach. I had a lifetime weight problem—just twenty extra pounds which made me feel uncomfortable with myself, enough to want to tell those pounds goodbye forever. I don't believe in diets. Diets are something people "go on" and <u>then</u> "go off." I wanted a lifetime change as dramatic as giving up cigarettes. I confronted myself in the mirror again—stark naked so I couldn't delude myself—and I talked positively to myself about being a thin person. I kept repeating, "I <u>am</u> a thin person," and eventually my subconscious begain to <u>believe</u> it. Food was no longer the emotional substitute it always had been. I gave myself true eye contact in the mirror and admitted that I had let food control me. Then I got in control and the twenty pounds melted off over a period of three years.

If you can get GROUP HELP for your addictions, great! You can talk to other people with the same addiction for positive feedback rather than spending so much time talking to yourself. The point is YOU CAN DO IT ALONE. We die alone, so we might as well accept that we must solve our own problems alone.

Whenever those little "goblins" in our heads start ganging up on us, telling us we need a cigarette, we are grateful that we have learned the art of "self-talk" and can fight back with a good argument, convincing us that we really don't need that cigarette . . . so we win again, and that is what success is all about—WINNING!

Please remember that the "goblins" in the head are just the old programs that our computer-brain has stored away under "Lost." They are stored away only until a stress situation comes our way, and then the "goblins" want us to have "just one cigarette for old time's sake." <u>Tell them to get lost again</u>. If you are willing to do this often enough, they'll get the message and find it less tempting to come out and tease you. <u>Convince</u> yourself that cigarettes never solved your problems anyway. They just covered them up, but they always resurfaced. The exciting thing is that without your cigarettes you'll learn to face your problems squarely. When they are in front of you, they no longer appear so frightening. You can begin to conquer them.

THINK ONLY SUCCESS FOR YOURSELF, AND SET YOURSELF UP FOR SUCCESS. Some people always experience failure. They never do realize that they <u>continue</u> to set themselves up for failure over and over again. Think SUCCESS, and you'll receive it. Think FAILURE, and you'll experience it. There are always exceptions, but this book wasn't written just for the exceptions.

If you can foresee a stress situation coming up, have a strategy planned so you won't go back to smoking. Some stress situations are unavoidable, but since they'll happen whether you smoke or not, why have stress situations and smoking on top of them? "Success is only one cigarette away, and so is failure!" Smoking your last cigarette is success and smoking your first is failure. Remember, after you have been off cigarettes for a LONG period of time and a STRESS situation comes up, it isn't the nicotine that tempts you—it is STRESS. (Reread the chapter on Stress Management.) The nicotine is out of your system and you are simply reacting to a trigger mechanism that has been activated. <u>Deactivate it quickly</u>. It is very difficult to accept that we solved our problems with smoking, but many smokers who refuse to believe this can't "make it" a day without nicotine. This is the problem!

I consider myself a winner in the stop-smoking game, but I had to go with a "winning team." I had to build that team—that team was myself. Build yourself up and you'll become a winner, too. It's your body, your mind, and your freedom. WIN IT BACK!!

"Every so often I slip back into reality and realize how <u>insane</u> I've been."—A <u>successful</u> ex-smoker during withdrawal period

A New Note on the Concept of Self-Righteousness

When I wrote the book 5 years ago, I was totally against any form of self-righteous thought or behavior. I am also continuing to learn and grow. I have some new insights on this concept I would like to share with you.

After becoming more honest with myself, I realized that I too often _felt_ self-righteous when I saw a smoker acting out a self-destructive habit—I just always prided myself on the fact that I never _said_ anything! Yet, the feelings were still there. My _Spiritual_ self would state, "I have no right to judge other human beings," yet my _Intellectual_ self would state, "But how can they continue to slowly kill themselves when they know better?" At the same time, my _Emotional_ self would state, "How dare they still have the pleasure that _my_ pleasure center still desires?" This conflict not only caused confusion, but guilt!

Always remember that self-righteousness occurs when we are in the process of _changing_ our belief or perceptions. When we have truly _made_ the transitions from BELIEF to _LIVING_ WHAT WE BELIEVE, there is little time for self-righteousness . . . we become role models.

Then last year I truly got educated when a family member went through a treatment center for alcohol/drug addiction. I saw that those who go through treatment centers (or stop-smoking classes) _need_ to have a sense of self-righteousness to stay sober or drug-free. That self-righteousness is the beginning of new belief systems and perceptions (see Stress Management chapter V.) they must develop to _survive_—to choose life over self-destruction! These new beliefs and perceptions can drive us crazy at first because they are stated so frequently and loudly—to everyone they meet. Any time we learn something new, we think the whole world should learn it, too! When I complained to my husband about the family member's self-righteousness, he stated, "Would you rather have her self-righteous or _dead_?!" How simple and how true!! This was my learning.

So when you _feel_ self-righteous, this is your will to survive fighting for you! You don't have to _act_ it out by always being rude to those who still choose to smoke. Just please remember, "HOW YOU FEEL IS ALRIGHT FOR YOU—YOUR FEELINGS ARE VALID. SO, ACCEPT THE SELF-RIGHTEOUS PART OF YOURSELF. THEN DECIDE HOW YOU CHOOSE TO ACT OUT THIS SELF-RIGHTEOUS PART OF YOU IN A MANNER THAT PROTECTS YOUR OWN INTEGRITY AND DOES NOT VIOLATE THE INTEGRITY OF ANOTHER. YOU CAN DO THIS BY TAKING ACTION AND SUPPORT OTHERS WHO CHOOSE TO QUIT SMOKING. . . . YOU CAN WRITE YOUR CONGRESSPERSON OR SENATORS AND LOBBY FOR WHAT YOU BELIEVE ABOUT THE SMOKING ISSUE. YOU CAN SIT DOWN AND WRITE A SELF-RIGHTEOUS, ANGRY LETTER TO THE PERSON WHO OFFENDS YOU—THEN TEAR IT UP! JUST GETTING OUR SELF-RIGHTEOUS FEELINGS DOWN ON PAPER RELIEVES MUCH OF THE TENSION. YOU CAN CENTER YOURSELF BY CLOSING YOUR EYES AND GIVING YOURSELF SOME QUIET MOMENTS TO REFLECT ON HOW FORTUNATE YOU ARE TO HAVE HAD THE MOTIVATION TO DO THE HARD WORK THAT IT TOOK TO GET OFF CIGARETTES. . . . AN ATTITUDE OF GRATITUDE. IT IS IMPOSSIBLE TO FEEL SELF-RIGHTEOUS DURING GENUINE FEELINGS OF GRATITUDE.

Summary on Self-Righteousness

1. Allow yourself the feelings of self-righteousness. Your feelings are always valid. Accept this part of you. Your action/reactions may not be valid—you have a <u>choice</u> in how you react/ act.
2. Decide how you intend to act out these feelings: constructively or destructively?
3. Choose an action plan to act out these feelings in a creative manner, such as starting a support group, supporting someone else in quitting smoking, taking an assertive stance and telling the person how you feel, writing letters to create action on the smoking issue, or writing an angry letter—THEN TEARING IT UP! Or getting counseling to help you through this issue. IT TAKES STRENGTH TO ASK FOR HELP!
4. And always remember that self-righteousness occurs when we are in the process of changing our belief or perceptions. When we have truly <u>made</u> the transitions from BELIEF TO <u>LIVING</u> WHAT WE BELIEVE, there is little time for self-righteousness—we become role models.

"May I never forget the control that Nicotine had over me. I was willing to DIE for Nicotine—and I almost did! <u>And Nicotine never cared about me</u>—Nicotine just seduced the next victim. . . ."
—Anonymous Ex-Smoker—5 years

XIV

The Three "C's" of Being an Ex-Smoker

*"Self-righteous ex-smokers compete with tobacco advertising to
keep smokers smoking."*—L. B.

You have now become an ex-smoker. You have declared that your health and self-respect are important to you; how will you now relay this message to those still smoking around you? Chances are you will no longer care to breathe stale cigarette smoke in enclosed areas in restaurants, in your car, in your own home. How can you let your friends who still smoke know how you feel without hurting your friendship with them? Please avoid "self-righteous attacks" as there is already a worldwide epidemic of this sometimes incurable "disease."

1. COURAGE
First of all, it takes courage to speak up for yourself. It takes courage to say, "I have worked hard to become an ex-smoker—please respect this." It takes courage to say, "I'm giving my lungs and heart a second chance; please respect this."

2. COMMUNICATION
The simplest way to relay this message is to post a THANK YOU FOR NOT SMOKING or NO SMOKING sign on your front door or your auto window. However, you cannot carry signs wherever you go; direct communication is often wiser. Communication means that two people, or two groups of people, achieve understanding; it does not mean that we alienate friends and neighbors over the issue of "to smoke or not to smoke." Communicate with tact and courtesy.

If your best friend still smokes, tell him/her that their friendship is very important to you. But part of that friendship was based on the companionship of smoking together. How are you going to replace the smoking companionship you had? Perhaps you could make a contract together with the stipulation that your friend not smoke in your home, auto, or when dining together, if you are willing never to nag or criticize his/her smoking habit.

If your friends test your relationship by lighting up a cigarette in your home, you could say, "It's nice outside, let's step outside together while you have your cigarette." If you're in your car, perhaps you could say, "Let me pull over at the next convenient stop, and I'll rest while you have your cigarette." Or you could let your friends know (right off and with much enthusiasm) how much you LOVE the smoke-free smell of your house, and you've promised yourself to keep it that way. If these ideas don't help, you must plan your own method of communication; it is best to have alternative ways to handle situations as people react differently themselves to given situations.

3. COURTESY
Please remember, all of us like to be treated courteously. There is much talk today about assertive behavior; the line is very thin between positive assertive behavior and negative aggressive

behavior. Assertive behavior says: "I believe in myself, my goals, and my rights." It is said with <u>courage</u> that is <u>communicated</u> with <u>courtesy</u> for the feelings and rights of others. This type of behavior cannot only influence others, but can perhaps give incentive to the other person to become an ex-smoker. Aggressive behavior says: "I'm not sure what I believe in, but if I behave rudely and loudly enough, perhaps I'll <u>fool</u> both of us." Needless to say, this only <u>alienates</u> others— making them feel like lighting up another cigarette. It also makes smokers feel trapped and they already are feeling trapped by their smoking habit. The more trapped <u>they</u> feel, the more they resent <u>your</u> freedom. Help them feel their freedom by making an agreement which works for both of you. Smokers feel very strongly about their smoking rights. Don't forget, it wasn't too long ago that this was <u>your</u> way of thinking.

<u>You have worked hard to achieve the goal of becoming an ex-smoker and you want to defend this achievement like a mother cat defends her litter of kittens.</u> But the reality still exists that cigarette smokers will always be in our world, many of them friends and potential friends. When you are unable to communicate your message successfully, vent your anger in <u>constructive</u> ways by writing your legislators and encouraging them not to support tobacco subsidies and to vote for more non-smoking areas in public areas. And thank those who already have non-smoking sections by writing letters or readatorials in your local paper.

GOOD LUCK!!

"Whenever I have that terrible urge to be self-righteous, I remember Linda telling me about the 'humbling man' and I change my self-righteousness to GRATITUDE—for I am one of the fortunate ones!"—An ex-smoker

Definition of Terms Used in the Book

SELF-RIGHTEOUS PEOPLE: People who will never let you forget they never "needed" to smoke. If they did ever smoke, they tend to suffer from "self-righteous attacks" when telling you how "easy" it was for them to quit. They do not seem to have PEACE OF MIND. We are tempted to give them a PIECE OF MIND! But we will control ourselves, lest we become self-righteous. In this book you will find me occasionally bordering on self-righteousness. Forgive me—I am not "Perfect People."

PERFECT PEOPLE: People so afraid of life and the opinions of others that they actually don't make many mistakes. If they do, they behave badly. They are not able to view mistakes such as smoking habits as learning processes. They cannot understand how Thomas Edison allowed himself 10,000 mistakes in the learning process of discovering the light bulb. They would have been afraid to try. Mistakes such as the smoking habit embarrass them. They are often really not as "strong" as they appear; they have not felt the pain of "weakness." When you quit smoking, "perfect people" will like you better. They will want to be your friend. Let them—THEY NEED YOU!

YOUR COMPUTER: Refers to your brain and the ability to train our thought process, and to choose "what goes in, and what comes out." If we can "program" ourselves to smoke, we can also "program" ourselves to quit smoking.

SUB-CONSCIOUS: That part of your mind programmed by constant repetition and belief. Through constant repetition, we can adopt any thought process—like the "smoking habit."

GOBLINS: The little voices in our heads that appear as friends. They will try talking you into having that "first cigarette" after you have quit. They are employed by BIG BOSS NICOTINE. You must learn to talk back to these little voices. You will not be declared insane if you do!

VISUALIZATION: Being able to close your eyes and "picture" something as you want it to be— like your being an ex-smoker. You can then learn to do it with your eyes open. It works if repeated. All successful people use this technique; it is not new. It has been around since the beginning of time. All children use it—someone just takes it away from them before they grow up. Then we need to learn it all over again. And it's fun!

BRAINWASHING: The tobacco industry uses this technique to encourage young people to smoke—just for "fun"—then one morning they wake up addicted. We will use brainwashing only in a positive manner. You will brainwash yourself out of the smoking habit.

Recommended Reading List

ALBERTI, ROBERT, Ph.D. & EMMONS, MICHAEL L., Ph.D. *Your Perfect Right: A guide to Assertive Living.* San Luis Obispo, CA: Impact Publishers, 1982.

BAILEY, COVERT. *Fit or Fat.* Boston: Houghton/Mifflin, 1977.

BAILEY, COVERT. *The Fit-or-Fat Target Diet.* Boston: Houghton/Mifflin, 1984.

BENSON, HERBERT H., M.D. *The Relaxation Response.* New York: Wm. Morrow & Co., Inc., 1975.

BENSON, HERBERT, M.D. *Beyond the Relaxation Response.* New York: Berkely Books, 1985.

BRAMSON, ROBERT M., Ph.D. *Coping with Difficult People.* New York: Doubleday, 1981.

BRIDGES, WILLIAM, Ph.D. *Transitions.* Reading, MA: Addison-Wesley Publishing Co., 1980.

BURNS, DAVID, M.D. *Feeling Good: The New Mood Therapy.* New York: Signet Books, 1980.

BUSCAGLIA, LEO F., Ph.D. *Loving Each Other.* New Jersey: Slack Press, 1984.

FRANKL, VICTOR, M.D. *Man's Search for Meaning.* New York: Pocket Books, 1963.

FRIEDMAN, MEYER, M.D. & ROSENMAN, RAY H., M.D. *Type A Behavior & Your Heart.* New York: Vawcett Press, 1976.

HALPERN, HOWARD M., Ph.D. *How to Break Your Addiction to a Person.* NY: Bantam Books, 1982.

HALPERN, HOWARD M., Ph.D. *Cutting Loose: An Adult Guide for Coming to Terms with Your Parents.* New York: Bantam Books, 1983.

JAMPOLSKY, GERALD, M.D. *Love is Letting Go of Fear.* Millbrae, CA: Celestial Arts, 1979.

JAMPOLSKY, GERALD, M.D. *Goodbye to Guilt: Releasing Fear through Forgiveness.* New York: Bantam Books, 1985.

KLAGSBRUN, FRANCINE. *Married People: Staying Together in the Age of Divorce.* New York: Bantam Books, 1985.

KRIEGEL, ROBERT & KRIEGEL, MARILYN. *The C Zone: Peak Performance under Pressure.* New York: Doubleday, 1984.

NORWOOD, ROBIN. *Women Who Love too Much.* Los Angeles: Jeremy P. Tarcher Inc. 1985.

PECK, M. SCOTT, M.D. *The Road Less Traveled.* New York: Simon & Schuster, Inc., 1978.

PELLETIER, KENNETH R. *Mind as Healer, Mind as Slayer.* New York: Dell Books, 1977.

PORTER, GARRETT & NORRIS, PATRICIA A., Ph.D. *Why Me?—Harnessing the Healing Power of the Human Spirit.* New Hampshire: Stillpoint Publishing, 1985.

SEYLE, HANS, M.C., Ph.D. *Stress without Distress.* Philadelphia: Lippincott Publishing Company, 1974.

SIEBERT, LAWRENCE ("Al"), Ph.D. & Associates. *The Survivor Personality [packet].* Send $4.50 to P.O. Box 535, Portland, Oregon 97207.

SMEDES, LEWIS B. *Forgive and Forget: Healing the Hurts We Don't Deserve.* New York: Harper & Row, 1984.

STERNS, ANN KAISER. *Living through Everyday Crises.* Chicago, IL: Thomas Moore Press, 1983.

VISCOTT, DAVID, M.D. *The Language of Feelings.* New York: Pocket Books, 1976.

VISCOTT, DAVID, M.D. *The Viscott Method: A Revolutionary Program for Self-Analysis and Self-understanding.* Boston: Houghton/Mifflin Publishing Co., 1984.

Recommended Music for Relaxation and Revitalization

<u>PACHELBEL CANON AND OTHER BAROQUE FAVORITES</u> . *(R.C.A. Recording Company. Maurice Andre/Paillard Chamber Orchestra)*

Pachelbel wrote this piece in 1760, which was the Baroque period in musical history. (Other period composers were Handel and Bach.) The rhythm of this piece lends an emotional and intellectual response to the listener. The "largo" rhythm is 60–80 beats per minute, attuned to the heartbeat and natural rhythms within our own bodies—a very self-unifying experience. <u>Pachelbel</u> and <u>The Fairy Ring</u> (listed below) allow you to feel centered . . . with yourself, your creator, and your world!

<u>Comments from Pachelbel lovers</u> : *I use it to release my emotional garbage after a stressful day • I put it on when the kids get home from school—slows us all down • we put it on the tape deck before we go to sleep • I use Pachelbel to intensify my retention while studying or reading.* Others report using it for background music while relaxing, centering, or praying.

<u>LARGOS FOR LEARNING, LOVING AND LIVING</u> . *(Plumeria Productions. Don Slepian. P.O. Box 54, Kailua, Hawaii 96734)*

This tape includes <u>Pachelbel Canon in D</u> ; Handel: <u>Largo from Concerto Grosso #1</u> ; Bach: "<u>Arioso</u>"; Vivaldi: "<u>Winter</u>" from Four Seasons; and more! This rhythm also inspires emotional release and intellectual stimulation. I (and others) use this for relaxation, self-facing, retention while learning, and just pure enjoyment.

<u>AUTUMN</u> . *(Windham Hill Records. George Winston, 1980. Piano—Largo)*

This tape—one of many that George Winston has produced and presented in concert at the Hult Center and worldwide—has been found to revitalize energy and to provide enjoyment. It has even inspired me (and others) to do our housework!!

<u>OMNI SUITE</u> . *(Steve Bergman Productions, P.O. Box 4577, Carmel, California 93921)*

Steve Bergman presents music that is soothing to spirit and soul; regenerates and revitalizes after a stressful day. For some it helps to "wind them down." Bergman also has a tape called <u>SUITE BABY DREAMS</u> for newborn babies. Send $8.43 for either tape to the above address.

<u>SPECTRUM SUITE</u> • <u>RECOLLECTIONS</u> . *(Halpren Sounds, 1775 Old Country Road #9, Belmont, California 94002)*

Dr. Halpren combines his scientific knowledge and musical expertise to create music that is "in tune" with the biological composition of the body itself. Listeners describe the music as "the kind of music you hear in your dreams."

<u>PEACEFUL EVENING</u> . *(Earthlight Center, Dept. 1, 13906 Ventura Boulevard, Sherman Oaks, California 91312)*

Composed and performed by David Gordon and Steve Gordon, this delightful tape is calming "environmental" music that remains in the background while you work, read, talk, or just take "time out" from a hectic day. Gentle instrumentals plus crickets, rain and other natural sounds. Send to above address for catalog of other "environmentals."

<u>THE FAIRY RING</u> . *(Mike Rowland, Sona Gaia Productions, 1845 N. Farwell Avenue, Milwaukee, Wisconsin 53202. [414] 272-6700])*

Gentle piano and synthesized strings create an almost magical effect. This tape is universally relaxing and revitalizing to our minds, bodies and spirits. . . . .ENJOY!

Diploma

_____ has survived
and graduated from

F. O. F.
School of Smoking

All credits & withdrawal honors
earned by graduate & applied
to Life, Health, Freedom & Choice

Calligraphy by MÆ '83 · Corvallis, OR

Awarded this date: _____
From a fellow scholar: Linda R. Bryson

Tapes and Book Available:

Rainbow Sunset

A 20-minute cassette by Linda which relaxes the entire body before taking you on a guided imagery trip to your favorite beach. Enjoy a beach sunset and listen to music while taking a break from stressful thoughts. This tape helps to quiet the mind and body, improve your coping skills and better your self-image and thought patterns.

$7.00 plus $1.50 postage

Stop Smoking

This cassette will help you to visualize yourself as a non-smoker and relax you so you may more easily resist those stressful and vulnerable moments when "just one puff" seems to be the answer. Play for 30 to 60 days as your own self-hypnosis course. By Linda Bryson.

$7.00 plus $1.50 postage

Weight Control

A 25-minute cassette by Linda which relaxes the body before experiencing the possibility of a healthy and thin self. Gives you positive affirmations to reinforce healthy eating patterns and positive self-images, plus two additional techniques to help explore and negate destructive eating patterns and habits.

$8.00 plus $1.50 postage

"What I Believe"   Louise L. Hay

This cassette elaborates on concepts of how we create our experiences in life. Side II is a deep relaxation and guided meditation to help you begin New Thought Patterns. Everyone can benefit from listening to Louise.

$9.50 plus $1.50 postage

Progressive Relaxation

This 30-minute cassette guides you as you learn to concentrate on relaxing tense muscle groups. You will experience the difference between tense muscles and relaxed muscles. By Linda Bryson.

$8.00 plus $1.50 postage

Are You Ready to Quit Smoking?

A workbook with universal techniques and tools to help eliminate the smoking habit more comfortably, sensibly and permanently. Can be used for other addictions, such as overeating, by applying the same techniques. 145 pages.
CHAPTERS ON:

- *Withdrawal*
- *Making Changes*
- *Support Systems*
- *Stress Management*
- *Women and Smoking*
- *Staying Off Forever*
- *Preparing for Quitting*
- *Sensible Weight Control*
  . . . and more!

$9.95 plus $1.50 postage
[Published by Kendall/Hunt Publishing Company, 1982]

To: **Linda R. Bryson**
28772 N.E. Karlene Drive
Corvallis, Oregon 97333
(503) 758-5137

Send order to:

NAME: _____

ADDRESS: _____

CITY: _____ STATE: _____
Zip

Order Form

	Quantity	Price Each	Total
Rainbow Sunset			
Weight Control			
Stop Smoking			
What I Believe			
Progressive Relaxation			
Are you Ready to Quit Smoking?			

TOTAL $ _____

Please allow 10 days for delivery

(Please make checks payable to LINDA R. BRYSON)